Turkey Hunting Tactics of the Pros

Books by Richard Combs

Canoeing and Kayaking Ohio's Streams (1983, 1994)
Advanced Turkey Hunting Tactics (2002)

Turkey Hunting Tactics of the Pros

*Expert Advice to Help You
Get a Gobbler This Season*

Richard Combs

The Lyons Press
Guilford, Connecticut
An imprint of The Globe Pequot Press

The Lyons Press in an imprint of The Globe Pequot Press.

Printed in the United States of America

Designed by Compset, Inc.

10 9 8 7 6 5 4 3

Library of Congress Cataloging-in-Publication Data is available on file.

Acknowledgments

Writers are often asked how long it took them to write a particular book. The stock answer, and probably the most accurate one, is "all my life." It is not possible to thank all the people without whom this book could not have been written, but I feel compelled to recognize some of them.

First, of course, I must thank the experts who generously gave of their time in contributing to this project. Their skill, experience, and dedication are reflected throughout the book.

I want to thank Jay Cassell and The Lyons Press for entrusting me with this project.

For their friendship and generosity in recent years I'd like to thank Joe Arterburn, Dave Draper, Cuz Strickland, C.J. Davis, Hank Strong, Russ Markesbery, and Chip Hart. We've shared a few campfires, and if I'm fortunate we will share at least a few more.

For his encouragement and support, I owe a special thanks to Mike Standlund, editor of *Bowhunting World* magazine.

Finally, I'm indebted to Steve Gillen, with whom I've shared not only quite a few campfires, but a good number of duck blinds, boats, and coverts, as well. I have benefited more than he knows from his expert counsel and advice.

For Hillary and Haley, the sun and the moon.

Contents

Introduction   1

1) Meet the Pros   5

    Paul Butski   5

    Peter Fiduccia   6

    Tim Hooey   7

    Dick Kirby   8

    John McDaniel   9

    Matt Morrett   10

    Larry Norton   11

    Steve Puppe   12

    Roger Raisch   13

    Eddie Salter   13

    Lovett Williams   14

2) Scouting   17

3) Run and Gun or Wait 'Em Out?   31

4) Weather or Not   41

5) Hunting Henned-Up Gobblers   51

6) Blinds   59

7) The Ultimate Challenge—Turkeys   71
    With a Bow

8) Optics for Turkey Hunters   85

9) Calling Secrets   97

10) The Perfect Setup   111

11) When the Woods Are Silent   121

12) Hunting the Slam   129

13) Afternoon Delight   141

14) Fall Turkey Hunting   147

15) Last-Ditch Tactics   153

16) Turkey Dogs   163

17) Wild Turkey Recipes   177

Index   185

Introduction

Perhaps chief among the things I value about my job as an outdoor writer is the opportunity to travel and spend time with people who have a passion for the outdoors and who are very good at what they do—whether it's drifting for winter steelhead on the Pere Marquette River, pulling stripers from the surf at Cape Cod, training bird dogs to point staunchly and retrieve to hand, or my own favorite outdoor pursuit—hunting wild turkeys.

Years ago, when my keen interest in turkey hunting was rivaled only by my lack of experience at this endeavor, I was invited on a hunt at a well-known lodge in Alabama. Attending the hunt was a veritable Who's Who of turkey hunting, including two world-champion turkey callers, several representatives of call, shotgun, and camo clothing makers, a couple of outdoor writers, and a number of experienced guides. The hunt was scheduled for three days, and for three days it rained seemingly nonstop. We spent chilly mornings in pickup trucks watching the black of night give way grudgingly to a dismal gray dawn as rain spattered the windshield and fog snagged in the treetops and we sat with our hands wrapped around warm mugs, sipping coffee and talking. Evenings we spent sitting on the veranda of the lodge in our stocking feet, boots lined up along the wall, listening to the rain as we sipped whiskey or beer or soda, and talked.

Mostly they talked, and I listened. They were all friends, and they were a jovial bunch, but in between all the ribbing and guffawing and knee slapping they reminisced about past hunts, discussed strategies for bagging henned-up toms, debated the merits of various shotguns and shotshells, argued about when aggressive hunting was most likely to fill a tag and when the situation called for a more patient, wait-'em-out approach, compared box calls, and generally hashed and rehashed nearly

Eastern turkey longbeard: What we're all looking for.

every imaginable aspect of turkey hunting. The guides argued about which of them had been saddled with the greatest number of incompetent turkey hunters, complete with highly detailed, if perhaps slightly embellished, anecdotal evidence. As a beginning turkey hunter I listened with particular care to this discussion, lest I end up as the inspiration for humorous anecdotes on some of their future hunts. I left for home disappointed with the hunting, but sure I had learned more about turkey hunting than if the weather had been fair and the hunting productive.

If there's a theme to this book, it must be that there's more than one way to kill a turkey. All the hunters whose methods are discussed in the pages that follow are consistently successful turkey hunters. And while many of them use similar tactics and strategies in various situations, you will see too that many of

The author poses with a Rio Grande gobbler.

them have different approaches to the sport, and some of them employ strategies that are diametrically opposed. In a similar vein, their understandings of wild turkeys and their behavior, what they do, and why they do what they do range from the simple, to the complex, to the highly imaginative. How to account for such a diversity of opinions and strategies among a range of such consistently successful experts? As I said, there is apparently more than one way to kill a turkey.

I invite you to picture yourself, as you read this book, sitting on the veranda of a hunting lodge in the evening, listening to the crickets and the tree frogs and the irregular patter of raindrops falling from the sodden leaves of a huge old oak tree onto the tin roof overhead as some of the best turkey hunters in the country talk about their favorite subject. Tomorrow is opening day, the rain is tapering off, the forecast calls for clear skies in the morning, and after a few hours of listening to these fellows talk turkey hunting tactics, you'll head for the woods with renewed confidence and a whole arsenal of turkey hunting tips and strategies.

—*Richard Combs*
March 2002

1

Meet the Pros

Paul Butski

Turkey calling and hunting is a way of life for this upstate New Yorker, known widely as the founder and owner of Butski's Game Calls. Butski's passion for hunting has taken him throughout the United States, from the Blue Ridge Mountains to the Rockies and beyond. One of the pre-mier callers in the nation today, Butski has won or placed in more than 150 turkey calling championships, includ-ing the Masters Invitational Open and the Levi Garrett All American Open. He was six times the U.S. Open Cham-pion and three times the Grand Na-tional Champion, and has also won the U.S. Open and Grand National Owl Hooting Championships. A life member of the NRA and the National

Paul Butski

Wild Turkey Federation, Butski is also on the pro staff for Hide-N-Pine camouflage. Butski has appeared numerous times on radio and television, including a live Saturday-night appearance at the Grand Ole Opry.

Peter Fiduccia

How does a boy from Brooklyn, whose parents don't hunt, grow up to be nationally known for his expertise as a hunter? It has to be in the genes. That's what Peter Fiduccia thinks, and in fact "It's in the Genes" is a chapter in one of the many books he has authored. Not only did Peter's parents not hunt, they wouldn't allow him to do so. He read outdoor magazines, joined the Outdoor Life book club, and read everything he could get his hands on about hunting and fishing. He didn't stop with fantasies and vicarious adventures, though—Peter began to board a bus in Manhattan to sneak out of the city to hunt and fish. (In those days you could carry a firearm on a bus!) His first turkey hunt took place in 1984 when, with Paul Butski, he bagged a gobbler and was hooked on the sport. Since then Peter has hunted turkeys from California to New England and most states in between.

Though perhaps better known for his expertise as a deer hunter and author of the highly successful *Whitetail Strategies*, Peter Fiduccia is an outstanding turkey hunter as well as a general all-around outdoorsman. A lifelong, dedicated sportsman, Fiduccia has devoted much of his life to sharing his outdoor knowledge and experience with other outdoorsmen. He has produced numerous award-winning television and video pro-

Peter Fiduccia

grams, including his own nationally syndicated television series, *Woods N' Water*. He's also known for the hundreds of magazine and newspaper articles he has penned for outdoor publications, and is one of the most sought-after speakers on the outdoor lecture circuit. Not surprisingly, given the important role that an outdoor book club played in his formative years, Peter is the founder and editor in chief of the Outdoorsman's Edge Book Club. He lives in the bedroom community of Warwick, New York, with his wife, Kate, an accomplished hunter, angler, and author herself, on a property surrounded by farms and mountains teeming with deer, bear, and, of course, turkeys.

Tim Hooey

I first got to know Tim Hooey on a hunt for turkeys and wild hogs at the Seminole reservation in Florida's Everglades, where we traveled to film a segment for Tim's *North American Fish and Game* television program. We stayed in chickees, the traditional thatched-hut dwelling of the Seminole. The temperatures were reaching into the low 90s, and one of the show's sponsors had sent us its latest camo clothing to wear—heavy stuff that would

have been ideal for a November morning in the Midwest, but was deadly in the Florida sun. While I pursued Osceolas with a smokepole and wild hogs with my bow, Tim was on the first leg of a quest that spring to take the Grand Slam with his bow.

What impressed me about Tim was his focus. He was relentless in his single-minded pursuit of his quarry. He hunted every available moment, and at the end of each day he did a

Tim Hooey

postmortem on the day's hunt and planned his strategy for the next day. Tim didn't score on our hunt, but as we left he was making plans to come back. Not surprisingly, he has since accomplished his goal of a bow Grand Slam in one season—in fact, he completed this slam in 28 days. An avid turkey hunter for more than 20 years, this former naval aviator has hunted turkeys in at least 21 states. Tim is a strong advocate for the National Wild Turkey Federation, and takes a special interest in teaching youngsters to be responsible stewards of our national resources.

Dick Kirby

What to say about Dick Kirby? The man has recorded 38 Grand Slams. Nineteen of those were in consecutive years, and he's planning for number 20 as these words are written. He has taken slams with shotgun, bow, muzzleloader, and pistol. In the spring of 1987 he recorded the first World Slam of turkeys taken in one season. I could go on about the other game he has hunted, but that's a subject for another book.

Space won't allow a complete list of his accomplishments. For many hunters the name *Dick Kirby* is almost synonymous with game calling, and rightly so. Founder and president (now semiretired) of Quaker Boy Game Calls, he has amassed an amazing record of calling titles over a span of 25 years, including world championships, U.S. Open Championships, Masters Invitational, and Champion of Champion titles. As recently as 2000, he won the World's Game Calling Championship, a calling contest in seven categories: turkey, owl, duck, goose, deer, elk, and predator.

Dick Kirby

Kirby is known not only for his accomplishments as a hunter, competitive caller, and successful businessman, but also for his strong support of conservation organizations including the National Wild Turkey Federation, the Rocky Mountain Elk Foundation, and Ducks Unlimited. He continues to devote much of his time to conservation activities, as well as to hunting and filming his adventures.

John McDaniel

John McDaniel is a guy you don't want to go turkey hunting with—not, that is, unless you are truly serious about turkey hunting. McDaniel's respect for the wild turkey and the hunters who pursue it ethically and with passion is matched only by the intensity with which he hunts. A professor of anthropology at Washington and Lee University, and author of several books on turkey hunting, including most recently *The American Wild Turkey* (Lyons Press, 2000), McDaniel compares the effective turkey hunter to a warrior, and the spring turkey season to a marathon. His family and colleagues in Virginia have learned that when the spring turkey season is on, he is going to be running on pure adrenaline, with little time for sleeping, eating, or engaging in social niceties.

Turkey hunting is not fun to McDaniel—the word *fun* would trivialize what for him is nothing less than a spiritual quest. Spiritual quests are not things to be taken lightly. As with all true quests, it is the quest itself, and not any result of it, that is important. A straight shooter—figuratively and literally—McDaniel pulls no punches in his disdain for hunters who cut corners, break rules, or show lack of proper respect for wild turkeys and their ethical pursuit. He

John McDaniel

approaches turkey hunting with an unusual mixture of pride and humility, and this, along with his experience and obvious knowledge of turkey hunting, is apparent anytime he addresses the subject.

Matt Morrett

Matt Morrett is from Pennsylvania—which, along with Michigan and arguably nowhere else, is one of the few places outside the South where hunting is a pervasive part of the culture. It's an eastern state, a mountain state, and a state featuring large tracts of public property. The hunting is excellent here, but it can be challenging. This is where Matt Morrett began hunting at the age of six, often tagging along with his father on scouting forays.

Not surprisingly for a young man growing up in a hunting family, his idols were Ben Lee, Dick Kirby, and the Rohm brothers, and his dream was to make a living in a hunting-related business.

Over the last decade or so Morrett has racked up an incredible string of calling championships, including world-champion friction caller (five times), U.S. Open Turkey Calling Champion (five times), and Grand National Champion. And those are just the major titles.

A member of the Hunter's Specialties pro staff, Morrett travels the country conducting seminars on turkey hunting and deer hunting, and helps design and field-test new products. He has appeared in numerous hunting videos, as well as on many outdoor television programs.

"I'm very fortunate to have the job that I have," Morrett acknowledges. "I have been privileged to hunt

Matt Morrett

turkeys and deer in some of the best states and areas available. My favorite hunting, though, is when I get to chase anything with my dad."

Larry Norton

Larry Norton is a tall, unassuming fellow from Alabama who walks from the hip in long, ground-eating strides like the true woodsman that he is. He also happens to be a two-time world turkey calling champion and a guide at Alabama's famous Bent Creek Lodge. Like most southern turkey hunters, Larry learned the fine art of turkey hunting as a youngster at his father's knee.

I've had the good fortune to hunt with him on several occasions, but the memory that stands out most vividly is the time we sat working a henned-up Bent Creek gobbler that approached in response to Larry's calls, then faded as his hens became agitated and called him back. This happened several times, and Larry listened intently to the hens each time. Larry decided the best strategy would be to back off and try this bird at another time.

That evening back at the lodge, he began making a diaphragm call, carefully trimming, pulling, and stretching the latex, yelping on it periodically and then readjusting. As a

Larry Norton

world-champion caller and a guide, he had a slew of calls, and I couldn't help but wonder why he felt the need, in the middle of Alabama's spring turkey season, to make a new one. Eventually it dawned on me—and he later confirmed—that he wasn't trying to sound like a turkey hen; he was trying to sound like *the* turkey hen—the dominant bird that had been yelping most aggressively to bring that straying gobbler back in line.

It would make a better story, I know, if I could say we went back to the woods the next morning and bagged that hen-pecked old tom. The next day was the last day of the hunt, though, and as it happened a thunderstorm washed us out. Larry will be the first to tell you that calling skills are only one part, and perhaps not even the most important part, of turkey hunting. Nonetheless, he has clearly taken the fine art of calling turkeys to a level few turkey hunters will ever approach.

Steve Puppe

As far as I can tell, two things are important to Steve Puppe: people, and hunting. A friendly, laid-back guy with a ready smile, Steve gives the impression of someone who is most at home in a hunting lodge. His relaxed demeanor and quiet sense of humor belie a real intensity about hunting. He might fish, play golf, collect Indian pottery, or fly model airplanes—I don't know. It's hard to imagine anyone spending any time with Steve,

Steve Puppe

though, and not learning that he's an avid hunter. The subject is going to come up, and it will probably be the only one about which he'll become truly animated.

A native of Minnesota, Steve is an excellent shot with a bow, and his prowess with a turkey call is widely respected. An outstanding public speaker and popular for his high-energy seminars, Puppe currently is a cohost of the *Outdoor Expeditions* television program. He lives with his family in Montana.

Roger Raisch

Born in Oelwein, Iowa, Roger Raisch participated in Iowa's first modern turkey season in 1975, and was hooked for life. An

Roger Raisch

avid deer bowhunter for years prior to that, he found that turkey hunting appealed to his love for intense, stealthy, high-quality hunting experiences. Roger has been chasing turkeys for more than 25 years now, and has enhanced his turkey hunting knowledge by spending thousands of hours hunting with bow and camera. For at least 15 of those years he has been sharing his turkey hunting strategies with others who want to become better turkey hunters. Roger has matched wits with wild turkeys from New York to Hawaii, with gun and bow. In an era when most of the literature dedicated to turkey hunting focused on the importance of patterning shotguns, the difference between a box call and a mouth call, and how to distinguish gobblers from hens, Roger's book *Turkey Hunting Secrets* discussed specific turkey hunting tactics and techniques, and its special emphasis on practical, effective methods for bowhunting turkeys has influenced an entire generation of bowhunters. A lifelong member of the National Wild Turkey Federation, and former president and director of the Iowa chapter of that organization, Roger currently hosts the popular TurkeyHuntingSecrets.com Web site, which includes an extensive library of turkey hunting literature as well as an online pro shop. Though he has lived most of his life in his native Iowa, in recent years he spends most of his time on his ranch in Missouri.

Eddie Salter

Eddie Salter is the turkey hunter's turkey hunter. Many a young turkey hunter—and more than a few not-so-young ones—called his first turkey to the gun with an Eddie Salter box call.

Like many southern turkey hunters, this Alabama native began turkey hunting as a youngster, calling in and bagging his

first gobbler at age 10. And though
Eddie is an accomplished deer hunter
and immensely enjoys waterfowl
hunting and other forms of the sport,
turkey hunting remains his first love.

I had an opportunity to bowhunt
for deer with Eddie a few years ago at

Eddie Salter

the Roost, a lodge with hunting prop-
erties straddling the Alabama–Mississippi line. The hunt took
place in October. A two-time world-champion turkey caller and
a Hunter's Specialties pro staffer, Eddie's a big man, and he's intense about hunting. His seriousness about hunting aside, his
warm, sincere nature and soft Alabama drawl have long made
his presence welcome at hunting camps throughout the South,
as well as in other parts of the country.

One evening, as we sat waiting for dinner at the Roost, the
name of another well-known turkey hunter was introduced into
the conversation.

"That boy is ate up with turkey hunting," Eddie said, shaking his head sympathetically. "He's just ate up with it." This
from a man who had been walking around the lodge on an October deer hunt gobbling and hen yelping with his voice.

Small wonder Eddie Salter is a fixture on outdoor television
programs, in hunting videos, and at hunting seminars.

Lovett Williams

Take a fellow who began a lifelong obsession with turkey
hunting as a lad in Florida 50 or so years ago. Throw in a doc-
torate in wildlife ecology, with a dissertation on the natural his-
tory of the wild turkey, and add to that a lifetime devoted to
studying, photographing, filming, and recording wild turkeys
year-round. Give him some experience in the public and private
sectors as a manager of turkey hunting properties, outfitter,

Lovett Williams

guide, and writer, and the result is predictable: a man who has forgotten more about turkeys and turkey hunting than most of us will ever know.

To put it another way, Lovett Williams's approach to turkey hunting combines the no-nonsense, just-give-me-the-facts approach of the trained scientist with the hunter's perspective of many years in the turkey woods. He has never claimed the title of World's Foremost Authority on turkeys and turkey hunting, but he gets my vote, along with (I suspect) the vote of thousands of other turkey hunters who learned much of what they know about calling and hunting turkeys from Lovett Williams's recordings of wild turkeys and the volumes he has written about his life-long love affair with America's biggest game bird.

Scouting

Infantrymen love the ground. They hike over it, sit down to eat on it, lie down to sleep on it, and, when danger threatens, embrace it. Perhaps I'm straining the analogy a little here, but I believe that good turkey hunters love the ground, too.

What's that got to do with scouting? Just this: The main reason for scouting, I propose, should be to become as intimately familiar with the ground—the lay of the land—as possible. The most effective turkey hunter is the one who knows every hill, knoll, drainage, creek bottom, logging road, fence, meadow, oak grove, ridgetop trail, and drainage in the area. When a tom gobbles at first light, the hunter who knows the lay of the land will know approximately where that gobbler is sounding off from—might even know which tree he's in. He'll know what's between him and that gobbler, which will give him a good indication of how closely to approach. He can make an educated guess about the bird's direction of travel from the roost, which will help him choose the right spot to set up and call from. He'll be aware of any obstacles that might hang the bird up, such as fences,

Scouting is a huge factor in turkey hunting success. Spot a bird like this in the preseason, and you'll know where to hunt.

streams, or ravines. A champion caller with excellent woods-manship skills will be greatly handicapped if he doesn't know the area he's hunting. A mediocre caller with only adequate woodsmanship skills will greatly boost his chances for success by simply knowing the lay of the land. Reading topo and plat maps, studying aerial photographs, and talking to knowledgeable locals can be of help, but there's no substitute for getting on the ground and walking every inch of it.

No doubt I'll raise the ire of some very good turkey hunters in saying this, but I'll say it anyway. For many beginning turkey hunters, scouting means mostly looking for turkey sign or turkeys themselves to ascertain that the birds are present in the area in huntable numbers, but with some exceptions, hunters should know that turkeys are in an area before they invest time in scouting it. There are quicker, easier, and more efficient ways of knowing that turkeys are in an area than scouting for turkey sign. Game wardens, wildlife biologists, other hunters, Internet resources, harvest statistics, and just plain local residents can probably tell you if good numbers of turkeys inhabit an area.

There's another important aspect of scouting that is about neither confirming the presence of turkeys nor learning the lay of the land, but patterning turkeys. If turkeys were truly predictable, hunting them would be much less challenging. Nonetheless, they do have favored roosting areas, favorite strut zones, dusting areas, and places where they tend to rest, or at least remain fairly inactive, at midday. Travel routes, activities, and general behavior vary from season to season, so it's important to understand what turkeys are doing, and where they're spending their time, come opening day. The best way to do this is to listen to them or observe them, quietly and from a distance, shortly before the season opens. One preseason morning spent sitting quietly and listening to gobblers on the roost, noting the direction they take when leaving the roost, and observing meadows, pastures, logging roads, oak glades, or forest openings can be invaluable. The hunter who is able and willing to spend several such mornings has probably done the single most important thing he can do to improve the odds of filling his tag—assuming, of course, that he has the basic knowledge, calling ability, and woodsmanship skills to hunt turkeys effec-

tively. The key is to avoid educating or alerting turkeys by calling to them, spooking them on the roost, or being spotted. And
yes, tracks, droppings, feathers, and other sign spotted on these
outings can be useful in learning where turkeys are roosting,
strutting, feeding, or dusting—though none of these things is as
valuable as hearing or seeing turkeys.

There's room for a lot of controversy about the best way to fill
a turkey tag, or for that matter the best way to go about scouting
for turkeys. Conditions vary from one region of the country to
another. Some hunters are chasing heavily hunted public land
gobblers over large tracts of forest, others hunt private timber
leases in the South, while midwestern hunters often hunt farms
of 200 acres or less. All these factors affect not only hunting strategies, but scouting strategies as well. For these reasons and other,
more subjective ones, our experts reveal a wide range of approaches to scouting for turkeys. All the experts agree, though,
that scouting is one of the more important aspects of the sport.

"Certainly scouting is critical," asserts John McDaniel.
"Hunters need to find new areas to hunt, and those areas need
to be scouted." McDaniel often hunts large tracts of public land,
and scouting efficiently is important.

"I think many spring turkey hunters waste time by returning to areas with which they're already familiar. They spend a
lot of time sitting and listening to turkeys in the morning, to
see where they're roosting and where they go. But if the turkeys
have been there in previous seasons, they're almost sure to be
there next season, and they'll probably roost in the same areas
and strut in the same areas."

McDaniel has hit on a system for scouting new areas that allows him to make the best use of his time, as well as to save energy
for the approaching season. He scouts mostly in the afternoon.

"Scouting in the afternoon is a lot less taxing, and I won't
be exhausted by the beginning of the season. I can learn the

*Turkey feather and hen droppings may indicate
that a roosting site is in the area.*

topography as well in the afternoon as in the morning, and the sign will be there to tell me turkeys are in the area and, more specifically, where the strutting areas are."

McDaniel does occasionally get out in the morning and listen to birds in new areas. The mountainous, heavily forested places he hunts don't lend themselves to glassing for birds, and he does very little of that.

McDaniel does a lot of fall turkey hunting, and he feels it's important to distinguish scouting for fall turkeys from scouting for spring turkeys.

"In the fall," he says, "turkeys are much more mobile, and they often use different food sources from one autumn to the next. If mast production is poor in a given area, for instance, turkeys will probably be elsewhere. Hunters need to scout the fall turkey woods to find where the food is and where the turkeys are."

Agriculture is not a real factor in the areas McDaniel usually hunts, but in many regions of the country it is. It stands to reason that rotating corn and other crops can be a major influence on turkey locations in these areas from one fall season to the next.

"A turkey hunter can't do too much scouting," insists Eddie Salter. "He has got to know the lay of the land."

Salter starts scouting for spring turkeys months ahead of time, sometimes as early as the preceding fall, but takes scouting more seriously beginning about a month before the season opens. By a week or two before the season, he's in full combat mode, locating gobbler roosting areas, spotting strut zones, and listening to the birds as they travel from the roost.

His approach to scouting is based on his conviction that turkeys are very patternable. This is not to say they're truly predictable, and certainly over time their habits change. Salter is convinced, though, that if undisturbed they tend to roost in the same areas, and strut in the same areas, for weeks at a time.

"I like to just listen to gobblers for half an hour or an hour after first light," he says. "Later, when I'm sure they've left the area, I like to go look at where they've been and figure out why they were there. Why did they roost here? Why did they go

Gobbler track—a sure sign that turkeys are using the area.

there? And how did they get from this spot to this spot, and why did they use that route?"

The great amount of time he spends aggressively scouting shouldn't be misinterpreted. He's very careful to avoid spooking birds or alerting them.

"I like to start in creek bottoms," Salter tells turkey hunters. "Often I'll wear rubber boots and wade, to avoid making noise. Sometimes I'll zigzag quietly through a creek bottom, mostly just listening. If there isn't a good creek to wade, I'll make use of logging roads or fire lanes to cover ground without disturbing turkeys."

Peter Fiduccia believes strongly in the importance of scouting, but warns hunters not to educate turkeys prior to the season. He practices what might best be termed minimum-impact scouting.

"I learn the lay of the land during deer season so I don't have to penetrate an area over and over again before turkey season begins. I do all my scouting, when it's practical, from the road. I only scout the woods when I have to."

Peter waits until midmorning to drive the areas he is scouting, when the birds are often feeding in fields. He takes care to park his truck at some distance, where it won't alert the turkeys, then glass them from a distance.

He does occasionally go into the woods, to locate roosting birds—not in the early morning, but in the evening.

"I select a spot that I can watch from a distance, and again, I glass the birds as they make their way to roost.

"I never use any type of call while I'm scouting. The first call I make is on opening day. I don't like putting pressure on the flock or wising them up before I hunt them."

I asked Peter specifically about the importance of scouting shortly before opening day. He agreed that it was crucial, but reemphasized the importance of not educating or spooking turkeys.

"I believe it's important to scout before the season, but as I mentioned, carefully. Don't exert pressure or make any calls, and especially don't scout the same locations several times prior to opening day."

Paul Butski encourages hunters attending his seminars to think of turkey hunting as a numbers game. It's all about doing everything you can to tip the odds in your favor, and it all goes back to scouting, because the more turkeys you have located prior to the season, the more birds you have an opportunity to work—and the better your chances.

"We have a lot of state land to hunt in my part of the country," says Butski. "My scouting for new turkey hunting spots starts in the fall. The birds are concentrated then in good numbers, and remain that way through the winter. Generally, if there are good numbers of birds in an area in the fall, there will be good numbers in the spring.

"Later, when the toms start to gobble, I have sometimes used a map to mark all the spots where I've heard gobbling activity. The idea is not to be rambling through the woods when turkey season arrives. You want to know where you're going and why."

Unlike many experts, Butski does call turkeys in the preseason. He starts with locator calls, but if these don't elicit gobbles, he'll move on to turkey calls. He's quick to point out here that he never attempts to bring birds in to the call. He simply wants to elicit that gobble, and when he gets it he quits calling and leaves the area.

"You don't want to play with that bird, and educate it," he warns.

He also cautions hunters not to assume that turkeys aren't there just because they don't answer a call.

Butski makes use of access roads whenever possible. This way, he feels, he can cover a lot of ground very efficiently while at the same time avoid spooking birds.

I asked him once if he attempts to pattern gobblers.

"No," he said. "Not unless I'm after a specific turkey. Then I'll try to pattern the bird to figure him out."

In areas that are entirely new to him, Butski does spend time on the ground just learning his way around.

For Lovett Williams, turkey hunting, properly done, seems to *be* scouting. He spends much of his time with his eyes to the ground, examining sign.

"Turkey hunting is like detective work," says Lovett. "The challenge is figuring them out. I gather information as I hunt, examining sign to figure out where the turkeys have been, what they've been doing, and where they're going. Eventually, you put all the pieces together and close in on them.

"Maybe I don't get a turkey on a given day, but I learn something. Let's say I see fresh tracks in a certain spot every time I walk by it. I know that's a hot spot.

"I get a peculiar kind of satisfaction in going out and killing a turkey right off the bat, early in the hunt. But that's not the most enjoyable kind of hunt to me. I'd rather hunt hard, and feel like I figured them out.

"In a similar way, sometimes you kill a turkey through luck. You just happen on the right spot at the right moment, and there he is. To me, a turkey that's taken through luck is a wasted turkey. I want to feel like I earned him."

I was particulary interested in talking to Lovett Williams about the extent to which turkeys can be patterned, since few people have spent as much time as he has observing and studying the behavior of wild turkeys.

"Yes, turkeys can be patterned," he says, "but it's not easy. I've put transmitters on them, and I can tell you they can be very irregular. At times they can be pretty regular, too. There's a certain probability associated with a turkey being in a certain spot at a certain time, and the probability is high enough to make sitting in a given spot worthwhile."

Roger Raisch is a meticulous record keeper and a firm believer in scouting. A dedicated hunter of fall turkeys as well as spring turkeys, Roger scouts year-round.

"I scout during four distinctly different time periods," he explains. "About a month before the season, a few days before the opening of the season, during the season, and postseason. Turkeys are behaving very differently during these time periods."

Roger keeps a journal of his scouting forays, noting weather conditions and number and gender of turkeys seen, in addition to feeding, roosting, and loafing locations, travel routes, and observations on behavior. Roger feels that his journal, along with a topo map on which he marks sightings and other information, is invaluable to him during hunting season.

A believer in patterning turkeys, Roger recommends that hunters scout ". . . until you feel comfortable that you know the daily patterns of turkeys.

"The patterns that turkeys are following just prior to your hunt are a much better indicator of what they're likely to do than observations you made on a scouting trip a month earlier. When you can piece together your scouting information from various scouting trips, patterns start to develop. Then you'll be able to predict where turkeys are likely to be at various times of the day, greatly improving your chances."

Roger agrees with most of our experts that scouting is less critical for hunters returning to familiar locations.

*Dusting area. Turkeys often return again and again
to an established spot.*

"When I hunt my favorite real estate in Missouri, I feel confident heading right to a favorite roosting spot, with no scouting whatsoever, and turkeys are usually there."

During the spring season, Roger often likes to spend afternoons scouting. In addition to roosting birds, he feels that observing the activities and behavior of gobblers can offer some clues on the best strategy for the following day's hunt.

In unfamiliar territory Roger covers a lot of ground just learning the lay of the land. He uses locator calls to make gobblers sound off, and will occasionally resort to hen yelping, but carefully avoids calling birds in. Generally he tries to be as stealthy as possible to avoid alerting turkeys to his presence. He listens to them and observes them from concealment to pattern them.

One specific tactic Roger employs when scouting is that of gaining altitude. He likes to climb trees, silos, windmills, or even buildings or other vantage points from which he can use binoculars or a spotting scope to observe turkeys over a large area.

"From a good location," he points out, "I often locate gobblers by themselves, in mixed flocks, or in gobbler-only flocks, observing their patterns and watching them go to roost with very little effort."

Roger points out that the patterns he observes usually hold up from year to year, with turkeys going to the same strut zones, feeding areas, or loafing areas each spring. He attaches special importance to strut zones, the open, often green areas where hens feed and gobblers strut.

"Good strut zones will produce year after year."

Run and Gun or
Wait 'Em Out?

Arguably this is the most fundamental question of turkey hunting, and I can think of several good answers to it. "Yes" comes to mind. "Both" is probably another good answer. The old-timers, as every turkey hunter has heard, advocated yelping several times on a box call, then putting it down and waiting for three hours. Some of the better-known modern turkey hunters have developed a reputation—often a reputation they have encouraged—for hunting tactics that seem to entail nonstop prospecting at a pace intended to cover a lot of ground quickly, loud and sometimes frenetic calling, frequent relocating on gobbling birds, and an arsenal of tricks that include aggressive tactics such as simulating gobbler fights or challenging dominant hens in the hope that they'll lead a gobbler into shotgun range.

In fact, I suspect both strategies are often misunderstood and overstated. Hunters should keep in mind that in some cases the old-timers hunted gobblers only in the fall. Taking hens or young-of-the-year birds in the fall is one thing; taking a gobbler in the fall normally requires extreme patience and limited calling. To the extent the old-timers hunted gobblers in the spring, I suspect the admonition to "yelp three times and wait three hours" was in most cases an exaggeration to make the perfectly legitimate point that when in doubt, patience is often the most effective tactic.

At the same time, modern turkey hunters like to make the point that hunters should not be afraid to call or to experiment with different approaches, and that there are times when firing up a gobbler or pulling out all the stops to get him in gun range is the best way to go. Hunting videos and television programs contribute a lot to the trend toward more aggressive hunting, too. Aggressive calling to birds that get fired up and come in quickly, strutting and gobbling all the way, makes for more dramatic footage than do hunts in which patient and infrequent calling brings in the sly old tom (or the timid young one) that will not respond to aggressive calling, and which sneaks in slowly and silently.

Consider, too, the fact that several days (or more) of hunting must be compressed into a 15-minute TV or video segment. The programs aren't intentionally misleading, but it's the nature of the medium that viewers see turkeys being brought to the gun every 10 or 15 minutes. The frequent result, I suspect, is beginning turkey hunters who wonder what they're doing wrong when the turkey woods don't produce suicidal gobblers charging their positions on a regular basis, and who respond to their lack of success by trying to cover more ground more quickly, calling even louder and more aggressively, and relocating more often.

I asked some of our pros the following questions:

"First, if you had to characterize your style of turkey hunting as either run and gun or wait 'em out, which would it be?

Second, why do you favor this approach, and third, if you sometimes use both approaches, what factors dictate how you hunt turkeys on a given day or in a given situation?"

An interesting pattern emerged, and while each of the hunters has developed his own style of turkey hunting, some generalizations can be made. First, all of them indicated that they were impatient hunters. All suggested that they simply felt the need at times to force the issue, to make things happen. This seemed related to confidence, in that all are confident that if they can get a turkey to respond to their calls, and to keep responding, they can move in on the bird and find a way to bring him into shotgun range.

At the same time, many of them seemed almost apologetic to be aggressive turkey hunters. They hunt aggressively, it seems, not so much because they believe it to be more effective in all situations, but because they enjoy this style of hunting. And all indicated that patience is an important virtue for turkey hunters.

Did I say many of our experts seemed apologetic about hunting aggressively? Eddie Salter is not one of them. A lot of folks think Eddie Salter *invented* run and gun turkey hunting. Certainly his name has long been associated with an aggressive style of hunting characterized by covering a lot of ground and calling excitedly in an attempt to fire up a gobbler and bring him in fast.

"I'm not lookin' for just any ol' turkey," Salter often says in his soft southern drawl. "I'm lookin' for a turkey that's ready to die."

Hunting as if there's a gobbler behind every tree, Salter hits the woods running and rarely looks back. A gobbler that's in no hurry is a gobbler wasting precious time, as he sees it. Chances are Eddie Salter's going to push the issue, either firing the bird up or moving on to find another, more workable gobbler. As a world-champion turkey caller who began turkey hunting as a youngster, he's pretty good at firing them up.

Salter's aggressive style emerged from two factors: his confidence that he can find a gobbler that is ready, as he puts it, to die, and the fact that he learned turkey hunting in an area with large tracts of land on which to hunt.

Of course, labels such as *aggressive* are relative. It would be a mistake to think Salter never backs off on his calling, or never spends time sitting in one spot. When hunting is tough, because it's late in the season and the birds have been pressured, or because of bad weather or other factors, Salter will take the time to work a gobbler carefully, calling less frequently and less excitedly.

"Sometimes," Salter once told me, "I might wait almost an hour for a gobbler to come in." As I said, it's all relative.

Among the hunters responding to these questions, Dick Kirby seemed most inclined to rely on patience, but as Dick explained it, that is a fairly recent development.

Aggressive tactics helped these hunters take a pair of gobblers.

"I *used* to be a run and gun turkey hunter," says Kirby. "But as you get older, your body will tell you it's time to hunt less aggressively."

Unlike his southern counterparts, Kirby cut his turkey hunting teeth in Pennsylvania, New York, and other densely populated states where hunting pressure is relatively high. Getting away from roads—and other hunters—has often been a priority in these areas. Then, too, these birds are often big-woods turkeys. The birds are there, but turkey populations are not concentrated in high numbers, and the birds are spread out. Both these factors dictate covering lots of ground quickly. Kirby has often used a leapfrog hunting tactic in these areas, in which he and a companion park in separate locations, with one hunter hiking from his vehicle to the next, then driving that vehicle to a predetermined spot to pick up the other. In this way the two hunters can efficiently cover large tracts of forest, evading the crowds near roads and parking areas while prospecting huge areas for birds.

Even on smaller tracts of land, with greater concentrations of turkeys, Kirby feels that early in the season, when gobblers are not yet wary or call shy, aggressive tactics that entail covering a lot of ground in search of a hot-to-trot gobbler is an effective tactic. In fact, anytime gobbling activity seems to be at or near a peak is a situation in which Kirby is inclined to favor aggressive hunting tactics.

In big-hill country Kirby likes to move along ridgetops and use high-volume calls, such as boat-paddle-style box calls. When he gets a response or two and gets a fix on the location of a distant bird, he'll try to cut the distance in half before calling again. He emphasizes the importance of calling regularly, though, to avoid any surprises.

Another situation in which Kirby favors an aggressive, ground-covering style of hunting is on windy days. The wind tends to conceal the sounds of the moving hunter, and to some extent even the hunter's movements are less visible. And since the turkey's gobbles might not carry far in the wind, covering ground is more important.

"There is no denying, though, that run and gun hunters bump more birds," warns Kirby. Later in the season, or anytime he suspects birds are heavily hunted and call shy, he favors a more careful, patient style of hunting with less aggressive calling.

Totally apart from the birds themselves, local conditions can dictate a more cautious approach. Small tracts of heavily hunted land are one such condition, but another is the kind of wide-open, high-visibility situation common in the West. Obviously, when birds can see half a mile and concealment is limited, the hunter who moves around to cover ground is likely to be spotted by sharp-eyed turkeys.

Weather, too, can be a factor here. Kirby believes that sudden cold snaps, especially in more southerly climates, can cool the ardor of most gobblers, during which time a patient approach is most effective. In fact, Kirby feels that anytime birds are quiet and little gobbling activity is evident, a patient approach is probably more effective than an aggressive one.

Finally, Kirby points out that intimate knowledge of an area can make a patient, less aggressive approach to turkey hunting more effective.

"If you know exactly where the birds are, and where they're going when they come off the roost," he suggests, "why run around and risk bumping birds or educating them?"

Having had the opportunity to hunt with Steve Puppe, I can attest to his subtle sense of humor. When it comes to hunting, though, he's all business—direct and to the point. Puppe readily confesses to having little patience when it comes to waiting out a turkey.

*Especially when you know the terrain, a less aggressive
approach can be deadly on wary gobblers.*

"I would rather go to a gobbling bird a mile away than sit
out a quiet bird that's in my lap," he once told me. His feeling is
that if a bird is gobbling, he's vulnerable. So long as he continues to gobble, he's giving away his location, and Steve is going
to take advantage of this vulnerability by moving aggressively
toward the bird. He's confident that if he can get close and keep
the bird gobbling, he can find a way to fool him. He does concede, though, that there's a time and place for more cautious,
patient turkey hunting.

"Some days," he explains, "nothing is gobbling. Then I use
the sit and wait method. Usually a gobbler will come to soft
calling even though he may not make a sound. This is just not
as exciting, so if there's a bird talking, that's the one going
home with me that day."

Anyone who has the good fortune to hunt with two-time
world turkey calling champion Larry Norton had best get in

shape—this long-legged Alabaman covers his territory in big, ground-eating strides. I found this out a few years ago when I hunted with Norton at Alabama's Bent Creek Lodge, where he guides. Accustomed to pausing from time to time to wait for my turkey hunting companions to catch up with me, I found the shoe on the other foot when I hunted with Larry. He doesn't fool around, and he doesn't let hills, swamps, or thickets delay his progress.

Norton has no qualms about his aggressive hunting style. He's looking for a gobbler that will get fired up and come in, and on more than one occasion during our hunt Larry walked away from toms that gobbled but didn't seem sufficiently responsive to gobble continuously or head in our direction.

That's not to suggest he won't relocate on a gobbler that seems interested but hangs up, or that he won't work a bird carefully and give him time to come in, but he does want to see some clear indication of interest pretty early on in the conversation. It's also fair to point out that the circumstances under which he hunts on his home turf at Bent Creek lend themselves well to aggressive hunting. Bent Creek covers many thousands of acres of prime turkey habitat, carefully managed, on which hunter numbers are carefully controlled. He can hunt huge areas with birds that are lightly pursued, relatively speaking, and the sheer number of turkeys in the area means that devoting excessive amounts of time to any one bird is probably not the best strategy.

Part of Norton's aggressive strategy entails choosing setups with high visibility.

"I want to be able to see that bird as far away as possible, and I want to watch him all the way in. That way I can see how he's responding to my calls, and I can see if there are hens or other gobblers with him, and I can see if something hangs him up. If he's not gobbling a lot, I know he's still there if I can see him. And if a hen does lead him off, or he loses interest or changes direction, I know it right away and don't waste time sitting in one spot calling to a bird that's not there."

One problem with such high-visibility setups is that if the hunter can see the gobbler, the reverse is also true, and turkeys are notoriously sharp-eyed. Norton dismisses this concern, confident that his camo clothing and ability to sit motionless will ensure that very few turkeys will spot him before it's too late. His feeling is that the advantages of seeing the bird all the way in outweigh the slight possibility of being detected.

Persistence would describe Norton's hunting style far better than would *patience,* but he does exercise patience when necessary. His first instinct is to move to new ground when birds aren't cooperating in one area, but if the weather's bad or the woods are silent, he sticks it out, sitting by a green field or logging road and calling intermittently. He's also not reluctant to leave a henned-up gobbler and come back to the area later in the day, or even on another day. Impatient he may be, but when he senses that the time is not right for a particular tom, he'll slip away and leave it undisturbed for a duel at another time.

What conclusions can we draw from all this? Most of our pros clearly favor an aggressive hunting style. At the same time, they seem to concede that in many cases this is because they find it more exciting. Bringing in a tom that's fired up, gobbling and strutting all the way, is the scenario every turkey hunter envisions, experts and beginners alike.

Still, not every situation is conducive to aggressive hunting. Smaller tracts of land, heavily hunted birds that are wary and call shy, and conditions that keep gobbling to a minimum all suggest a more cautious, patient approach. By contrast, hunters fortunate enough to hunt big areas, with good populations of less pressured birds, may do well to pursue their quarry more aggressively. Each hunter must decide for himself when the circumstances warrant a given approach. The age and physical condition of the hunter are factors, too. Like Dick Kirby, I find myself, in middle age, gradually adopting a more patient approach to turkey hunting—less likely to hike down the hill, cross the valley, and climb to another ridgetop in response to a faint gobble in the distance; more inclined to seek the spots that turkeys frequent and wait them out. I can't say I bag more turkeys than I did when my legs were younger and stronger, but for what it's worth, I'm not taking fewer birds, either.

Perhaps the best tip we can take from the pros here is this: Turkey hunting, properly done, is an exciting sport. Whatever approach you take, when you have to start reminding yourself that turkey hunting is supposed to be fun, it's time to try a different strategy.

Weather or Not

A black, starless sky gave way slowly to a low, threatening cloud cover. I pocketed my flashlight and worked at matching strides with a famous turkey hunter as the muddy red clay of an Alabama logging road sucked at our boots. Fortunately, I had packed my rain gear.

"I see you're optimistic about the weather," I whispered as we stopped to examine some fresh tracks. "I noticed you don't have any rain gear on."

He shrugged. "A little drizzle won't bother me."

"What if it really rains?"

"When I'm hunting and it really rains," he said with a smirk, "I go home."

I could see his point. A wool jacket, or even a tree with foliage overhead, will turn a drizzle or light shower. And if it's pouring rain, the game won't be moving anyway, and a hunter is probably wasting his time in the woods.

On the other hand, there are only so many turkey seasons in a lifetime. And all but a fortunate few of us are limited to

*Snow squalls can reduce gobbling activity; unless
there is a real blizzard, however, turkey patterns should
remain relatively unchanged.*

hunting weekends and precious vacation time, making an already short period of time seem even shorter before the end of
another season rolls around and we're forced to hang up the
shotgun and wait for next year. A deluge is one thing, but spring
weather in particular is fickle, and if we let less-than-ideal conditions keep us out of the woods, our season can easily be short-
ened to little or no time at all.

The question is, how do we hunt effectively in rain, wind,
snow, or unseasonable temperatures? We know the turkeys are
still out there, somewhere, but where? We know their behavior
is likely to be affected by various weather conditions, but how?

There's no doubt that heavy rain, strong winds, snow, or
cold fronts can reduce gobbling activity, or limit feeding and
travel, but in all except extreme conditions turkeys are probably
less affected by weather than are hunters. Our own behavior is

probably a bigger factor than that of the turkeys when it comes to filling turkey tags in less-than-ideal weather. Obviously, we can't fill a tag if we stay home. Beyond that, though, our chances of success are greatly diminished if we let weather shorten the duration of our hunt, if we lose confidence, or if we're less alert in the woods because of discomfort or a perceived lack of activity among the turkeys.

Comfort is the real key—the hunter who's too wet, too cold, or too hot is going to be a less effective hunter. And staying comfortable under a wide range of conditions is largely a matter of having the right gear and using it properly.

It's hardly a news flash to outdoorsmen that layering is a key to comfort, but this is especially true for spring turkey hunters. Through most of the country in April and May, early mornings are chilly enough to require jackets or even long johns. By nine o'clock or so, the sun is getting high and the hunter is getting uncomfortably warm. A day pack into which hunters can stuff heavier shirts, jackets, or even the long johns is often a good idea.

Staying warm usually requires staying dry, and that means quality rain gear. Rain gear options have never been better for hunters. Quiet, breathable rain gear in camo patterns is widely available. It's not inexpensive, but it's worth every penny. Cheap rain gear is noisy, and since it doesn't breathe, it's hot and clammy.

Though you don't see it often in the spring turkey woods, wool is a great fabric for cold-weather turkey hunting. It's quiet, its insulating properties are unmatched by anything but down, and it turns rain well enough to keep hunters dry on drizzly days or in light showers.

Finally, the right boots are important. I've learned to keep three pairs. One pair is 17 inches with a leather top and rubber

An early morning shower didn't deter this hunter. The birds were active and vocal as soon as the rains subsided.

bottom. These are uninsulated but are sufficiently warm for all but the most bitterly cold weather. They're great for wet, muddy conditions, and wading creeks. For heavy-duty wading in swampy areas, all-rubber boots are the way to go, though they're clammy, hot, and not the best hiking boots in other conditions. Finally, I keep a pair of camo sneakers for hiking the hill country when conditions are dry. I exercise a little extra caution in them because their ankle support is probably inadequate for rough country, but they're extremely lightweight, cool, and comfortable.

I asked our experts, including John McDaniel, Peter Fiduccia, Roger Raisch, Larry Norton, and Eddie Salter, for their opinions about how various weather conditions affect turkey behavior, and how hunters should adjust their tactics for rain, snow, wind, or unseasonable temperatures.

"It's true turkeys don't gobble as much in cold weather," concedes Eddie Salter. "But hunters should remember that the breeding season is short. Gobblers have been waiting for it for ten months out of the year. They still want to make hay while the sun shines—even if the sun isn't shining."

Eddie emphasizes two things when it comes to hunting turkeys in poor weather, and the first is extra patience. When Mr. Run and Gun himself advises patience, the advice is worth serious consideration.

"Often, when conditions are poor and there isn't much gobbling going on, I'll ease carefully into the woods and use a blind, or make one. Then I'll start calling every 15 minutes or so. I'll continue to do that for an hour, maybe a little more, then I'll move quietly to another spot and do it again."

I'll have more to say about blinds in the chapter devoted specifically to that subject, but it's worth mentioning here that good blinds offer the obvious advantages of additional warmth in cold weather, and most afford at least some shelter from rain. (Those that don't can be treated.) In addition, the less ideal the weather, the more difficult it is to sit motionless for long periods. A blind allows considerable latitude for movement. The hunter in a blind can even drink a hot beverage while hunting. Anything that keeps us in the woods longer, more alert and more confident than we might otherwise be, is a valuable accessory. (On the flip side, fully enclosed blinds tend to get hot fast in mild conditions when the sun is shining on them.)

The other factor Eddie Salter emphasizes for successful poor-weather turkey hunting is scouting.

"A lot of times, gobblers won't go very far from the roost in bad weather. It helps a lot to know where they roost.

"It also helps to have a number of gobblers located in a number of spots. You don't want to put all your eggs in one basket and hunt one gobbler, or one spot, in bad weather. Ideally, you want be able to hunt one spot for an hour or so, then move to another spot, and so on."

"A thunderstorm moving in can be great for turkey hunting," contends Larry Norton. "The thunder will locate 'em. I've killed several turkeys that gobbled at thunder. You've got to be careful about lightning, though. You don't want to be sitting under a tree when there's lightning. When that starts, it's time to head for the truck."

Larry's strategy for taking turkeys in the rain is to head for the open spaces, since that's what turkeys generally do. Like his fellow Alabama native Eddie Salter, Larry believes that scouting takes on particular importance when bad weather makes the hunting tough.

"I'll go to fields, or to logging roads or even deer trails that are near fields, where I've seen tracks in the past. The turkeys will usually use the logging roads or trails to get to the fields.

"Turkeys aren't usually very vocal in this kind of weather, and this is no time for aggressive calling. Just call quietly a little every few minutes. If it's windy, you may have to call louder to be heard. I'm not really trying to fire up a gobbler in this situation, I'm just trying to catch one that's heading for the open anyway. The only reason I'm calling is so that if he comes out on the road going the other way, I might turn him around and bring him my way. It all goes back to scouting, though. I've killed several turkeys in situations like this, where I've found their tracks several months earlier."

A front moving through bringing unseasonably cold temperatures can shut gobbling activity down completely. Some hunters believe this has a greater effect on birds in more southerly climes, but it can have a negative impact anywhere.

"Here in Alabama, when we get a few days of very cold weather, which sometimes happens in the first week of the season, the turkeys stop gobbling and seem to break up into separate flocks of gobblers and hens. They may sometimes intermix a little, but they don't seem to have much interest in one another. When this happens, a hunter just about needs to resort to fall hunting tactics. I try to scatter a flock, and then make gobbler clucks and yelps with a box call to bring 'em in. It takes a lot of patience."

"Severe wind, rain, or snow will restrict turkeys' movements somewhat and prevent much of their calling from being heard by a hunter," concedes Roger Raisch. "Toms gobble much less frequently in these conditions than on a quiet, sunny day."

Nonetheless, he points out, "They can't go home and curl up around the fireplace."

Despite the weather, Raisch has observed that in less extreme conditions, turkeys go about their daily patterns in wind, rain, snow, or heat. He believes that the need to feed can drive them to brave almost any weather conditions.

"For example, I've watched spring gobblers strutting around and gobbling in gale-force winds, following a feeding flock of hens around out in the open."

When resting, turkeys like to seek protected areas in bad weather.

"On a windy day, I take a position on the lee side of a ridge where I can hear well and where my calling can be heard," says Raisch.

He agrees with others that turkeys tend to stay on the roost longer in rainy weather, but is convinced that sooner or later they will fly down and go about normal activities. He notes, too, that turkeys tend to seek fields or mature, open woods in the rain.

"My hot-weather experience indicates that spring turkeys will go through their daily feeding patterns normally, but will hole up in the shade during the rest of the day. The shade could be under a large tree in the open, or deeper in the woods, in a low-lying area where it's cooler."

Finally, Roger emphasizes the importance of not giving up in poor weather, reminding hunters that a bad day hunting is always better than a good day working.

"Find a good strut zone that's protected from the weather," he advises, "and stick with it for the best chance of success on a gobbler during bad weather in the spring season. I've bagged gobblers with gun and bow in every weather condition imaginable, at all times of day. Great patience, conditioning, and confidence are required to endure wild weather in the pursuit of a wild turkey. Consistent success can be had in all weather conditions, but not on every day."

John McDaniel is not the kind of turkey hunter to let a little weather stop him, though he concedes that wind can put a real damper on turkey hunting success.

"High winds can be an almost insurmountable problem," he says. "Apart from that, turkey hunters have great success in poor weather. Rain can make for very productive turkey hunting—uncomfortable, but good. One problem with rain is that hunters often have problems with their calls in wet weather."

Mouth calls, of course, are not affected by rain, and that's one of their advantages. Hunters using box calls and some other friction calls sometimes avoid getting them wet by carrying them in plastic bags, such as bread bags, and the calls can actually be operated without taking them out of the bag and exposing them to the weather.

McDaniel makes an interesting observation about poor weather that more turkey hunters would do well to keep in mind.

"Bad weather usually means decreased hunting pressure," he points out. That can be an important consideration for hunters chasing public land turkeys.

"If you wait for perfect weather, you're going to miss a lot of days afield," exhorts Peter Fiduccia. "I've never seen turkeys drastically alter their routine during a rainstorm or on a windy day."

In fact, there are times when Peter is convinced gobblers are easier to call in during the rain.

"I've noticed that gobblers will remain on the roost longer in rainy weather, if there are no hens on the ground." He points out, too, that heavy fog can have the same effect.

"Rain also drives birds into the fields and other open areas more quickly," he observes, suggesting that hunters should plan their strategies with this in mind.

"I don't think heat or snow plays any real role, either," he adds.

Peter's advice to turkey hunters is to be prepared for bad weather and keep hunting.

"Keep your calls and chalk dry in a plastic Ziploc bag," he advises. "I also like to use a hot seat that won't absorb moisture during bad weather."

Hunting Henned-Up Gobblers

I doubt I can convey the essence of spring turkey hunting any better than did my daughter at the age of four. Having overheard more than a few conversations about turkey hunting, and after asking a few questions to satisfy her curiosity, she explained it this way to a playmate: "My daddy tries to figure out where boy turkeys want to go. Then he goes there first and tries to sound like a girl turkey."

That pretty well sums it up, I suppose. As is the case with most kinds of hunting, it's all about being in the right place at the right time. A little knowledge, experience, and scouting can lead us to the right places, which is where turkeys go to strut, to eat, to dust, or to rest in the shade, or the routes they use in getting from one of those places to another.

Timing, though, can be a little trickier. Ideally, we want to be in the turkey woods when the gobblers are lonely. For three seasons out of the year, gobblers seem to need little in the way of companionship. Many of them form bachelor groups of two or three or more birds, but these seem to be loose aggregations, and if separated, gobblers normally seem to be in no hurry to rejoin the group—which is what makes fall gobbler hunting so challenging.

In late winter or early spring, depending on the latitude, gobblers begin displaying, gobbling, and fighting, seemingly more to determine dominance than for any other reason. In any case, well before the hens are ready for mating, the toms begin gobbling to them, reaching a peak shortly before actual mating begins. Gobblers are vulnerable to calling then. They're accustomed, of course, to the hens seeking them out when they gobble, as opposed to the other way around; this, and their sharp eyes and natural wariness, makes them challenging to hunt anytime. Still, lust can sometimes cause them to abandon much of their natural wariness and proceed quickly in the direction of any sounds resembling a hen, often gobbling and strutting all the way.

At some point hens begin responding, moving toward toms when they gobble on the roost, or later on the ground, and spending increasing amounts of time with them. With the need to attract hens diminished, gobbling activity is often limited to early mornings on the roost, and some gobblers don't gobble much even then.

Eventually, hens begin sneaking off later in the morning to their nests, and soon fewer and fewer of them respond to gobbling at all—at which point the gobblers get lonely and a second gobbling peak occurs, when the gobblers are once again more vulnerable to calling.

Of course, gobblers don't consult calendars. Peak gobbling periods will vary by at least a few days from year to year, and often by more than this. Weather is a major factor here, too. Hard rain, unseasonably cold weather, and hunting pressure

This nice bird was taken during the second gobbling season.

can all affect gobbling activity and, perhaps to some degree, mating activity.

When that magic time right before hens respond to gobbling, or after most of them have been bred and are sitting on their nests, coincides with the hunting season and with reasonably stable weather conditions, the hunting is easy—or at least as easy as turkey hunting gets.

When hens are with the gobblers, though, it's usually tough hunting. And since the spring season is short, and few hunters have unlimited amounts of time to spend afield, the best time to go turkey hunting is often whenever we can. This means we're sometimes going to be hunting henned-up toms. An old saw suggests that if there are too many cures for an illness, there really is no cure. If we're lucky, the same does not hold true for the malady of henned-up gobblers, because every experienced turkey hunter seems to have a different "cure" for the problem. Let's take a look at the cures prescribed by our experts.

One commonly prescribed formula for bringing in henned-up toms is to challenge the dominant hen. Get her riled up enough with aggressive hen calls (or so goes the theory) and she'll respond by seeking out her challenger, often bringing one or more gobblers with her. Larry Norton is skeptical of this approach.

"The gobbler will follow her, all right," he asserts. "But she won't be going in your direction. Far more often, when you threaten the hen, she's going to lead that gobbler off in the opposite direction." Larry prescribes different medicine.

"Bringing in a henned-up tom is hard to do," he concedes. It is possible, though, and Larry's approach is almost the opposite of challenging the hen.

"The trick," he says, "is to get close to the birds and call quietly." Larry believes that soft, reassuring calls stand a better chance of leading a hen in your direction, possibly because she accepts these calls as emanating from her own flock.

It's important to understand that by *close* Larry is not advocating that hunters attempt to stalk within gun range of the birds—a low-percentage tactic, not to mention an unsafe one. *Close* is a relative term, of course, and will vary depending on how well sound carries under given conditions, how thick the foliage is, and the extent to which the terrain affords concealment. If a hunter can move in close enough to the birds, giving full consideration to safety issues, that his quiet purrs, clucks, whines, or scratchings can be heard, he stands a better chance of bringing in the hen, and any accompanying gobblers.

Larry's fallback strategy? Mark the spot, slip away quietly, and plan to come back later in the morning, or even later in the season.

"Getting a hen into an argument is very effective, *if* you can do it," suggests John McDaniel, clearly implying that he sees this as a low-percentage tactic. McDaniel believes patience is an important ingredient in successfully hunting henned-up toms, but by *patience* he doesn't mean sitting in one spot forever.

"Moving on gobblers is key in this situation," says McDaniel. "Lots of times I leave henned-up gobblers, and return later. I think it's a mistake to sit and go through your whole repertoire of calls. You have to recognize that some birds won't come in no matter what you do."

In a similar vein, McDaniel thinks many hunters call too aggressively.

"Don't burn an area out," he advises. "Don't educate turkeys. In the long run, low-key calling is usually more effective."

Tim Hooey makes no bones about his approach to henned-up gobblers.

"I bushwhack 'em," he says matter-of-factly.

Hooey feels that while challenging the hens—hammering them, as he puts it—can sometimes work, far more often than not it doesn't. Instead, Hooey patterns the birds carefully.

"Turkeys are very habitual creatures," he explains. "They have a daily routine. Sure, they move around to different areas. They might have two or three different feeding areas or strut zones, two or three different roosting areas, and so on, but over time they tend to frequent these few areas, and usually they're at these areas around the same time each day. I glass 'em and study their habits.

"Then I go in and find them on the roost. I don't call to them on the roost. When they fly down, I'll use a locator, or an occasional soft yelp. I'm not trying to call the birds in, I just want to get a response so I can track them and figure out where they're going. As soon as I think I know, I loop around to get there first."

Hooey emphasizes the importance of making a very big loop to avoid alerting the birds or altering their destination.

"Patience is the key," he continues. "I sometimes put out a decoy, and then I wait. Only when they get close will I call, and then it's usually a little soft yelping, clucking, or purring. If I'm lucky, they'll come on the run when they spot the decoy. Other times, it's a matter of just waiting until they get there.

"This approach has worked for me time and time again. It doesn't always work, but percentagewise it's a much better strategy than challenging the hens."

Hooey made one other observation on this topic.

"If you're hunting an area that you've hunted often and know very well, you can probably skip the glassing and patterning. Chances are you know where the turkeys roost, feed, strut, and just plain hang out. In that case, just set up in those spots and wait. If they don't show up today, they'll probably be there tomorrow."

Steve Puppe, like many turkey hunters these days, is a believer in the "challenge the hen" approach. And though some hunters find this a low-percentage tactic, perhaps it's only fair to point out that *every* tactic is a low-percentage tactic. Any tactic that wasn't would probably have to be illegal. Puppe's strategy is to locate the birds on the roost, slip in close, and call aggressively to fire up a hen.

"I like to get within 75 yards of the roost, or even closer if the terrain and foliage allow. Most of the time," asserts Puppe, "they will fly down and land in your lap."

Lovett Williams, true to his background as a scientist, is a skeptic. He observes turkey behavior and, as a hunter, responds to it and attempts to predict it, but is reluctant to explain motives for fear of projecting human characteristics onto birds. This is not to say that good hunters don't come up with tactics that work for them, he concedes. But when hunters begin explaining the motives for behavior, they get into the realm of the imagination.

"For one thing, who's to say there's such a thing as a 'dominant hen'?" asks Williams. "I don't know if there's such a thing as a 'dominant hen' or not. And if a hen does come in to a hunter's calls, how do we know it's because she's mad and looking for a fight?"

Lovett has his own strategy for dealing with henned-up gobblers.

"Hunting henned-up gobblers is one of the few times I stalk turkeys," he says. The trick is finding them, since they often don't gobble much when henned up. Still, they're often part of a large and noisy group.

"A gang of turkeys makes a lot of noise. The jakes that are often part of these groups are especially noisy, and often you can hear them."

What about all those wary eyes and ears?

"Well, it's not easy," he admits. "But the noise they make helps, and in a group they tend to be preoccupied with one another. With plenty of concealment or the right terrain, a hunter can sometimes crawl in fairly close.

"You almost have to bushwhack 'em," he continues. "Figure out which way they're going and get ahead of them."

And if you have trouble locating the birds?

"Then you might have a bad day."

Blinds

For years I've had a love–hate relationship with hunting blinds. On the hate side, I've had blinds that were big, heavy, and extremely awkward to carry through the woods. I've had noisy blinds and blinds that rattled, shook, or even tipped over in the slightest breeze. I've had blinds that required an instruction manual, two patient people, and plenty of time to set up. I've had blinds that were too small, and some that were too big. I've had blinds that were perfect in every way except the windows were too low to shoot through and the low walls left no option for cutting new ones that were higher. I've had blinds that were 1 inch too short for me to fully stand up in. And every blind I've used has been unbearably hot soon after the sunlight hit it.

On the love side, blinds have enabled me to sit comfortably and observe, photograph, or shoot turkeys (and other game) at close range. They've offered warmth when it was cold, and kept me dry in the rain. I have often, without disturbing approaching game, sipped coffee in blinds, read in blinds, stretched my back in blinds, rubbed my eyes, swatted bugs, scratched where

*Author Richard Combs with a bow-killed turkey. The blind
helped him stay totally concealed.*

it itched, and even fixed wedgies in blinds. When it comes to turkey hunting, where scent is not an issue, there is very little a hunter can't do in a blind except make a lot of noise.

Remember that time the gobbler hung up about 60 yards out, pinning you down with your gun to your shoulder? How he strutted around, stopping to peck now and then or to gobble, but refusing to come a step closer? How your neck got stiff and your arm got so tired it began to ache, and how that drop of sweat ran from your armpit down your side and nearly drove you crazy? And that root under your tailbone that wasn't there before, remember that? And all the time, your bladder was swelling to unhealthful proportions.

Well, forget all that in a blind. In a blind you sit in a chair— one with arms if you want. You watch the bird making his way in, and you call as you think appropriate. Might as well pour a little more coffee, he's taking his time. Let's see, where did you put that little scratch box you've been wanting to try? This would be a good time for a few quiet little purrs. Finally, when you're confident he's in range, it's time to casually pick up your shotgun, take aim, and let the hammer down.

When they work, blinds almost feel like cheating. Almost.

They've gotten better in recent years, too. Blinds are available today that are light, compact, and fast to set up or take down. They conceal better, and they offer more windows, peepholes, and shooting ports. The better ones are quiet, reasonably sturdy, and don't flap in the slightest breeze.

Camo netting covers the windows in some blinds. Game doesn't see through it; hunters can not only see through it, but shoot through it, too.

They're ideal for youngsters, who can fidget to their hearts' content and even talk a little if they keep it to a whisper. Youngsters aside, blinds are a great way for two or more people to hunt together. Without the blind, the fact that two people are moving

Blinds are perfect for kids and beginning turkey hunters.

and making noise instead of one, along with the inevitable need to communicate, either vocally or with hand signals, is a real handicap. Inside the blind, this is not a problem. Two can hunt as effectively as one from the total concealment of a good blind.

Obviously, I have a bias toward relatively large, commercially produced, fully enclosed blinds. Not everyone thinks of blinds in such narrow terms. Hunters have been using blinds of one sort or another since the first primitive human hid behind a rock. Hunters still make use of natural blinds, or "hides." And then there are blinds consisting of two sticks with camo fabric stretched between them. There are even waxed cardboard blinds that are surprisingly durable. These blinds can be useful, hiding the movement required to work a friction call, if nothing else. The problem I have with these blinds is the fear that (a) the gobbler will approach from behind or from an open side, and (b) without a roof and a dark interior, the blind will allow sharp-eyed turkeys to spot movement through shooting ports or over the top (if the blind requires me to shoot over its top). As we'll see, though, some experts make effective use of all kinds of blinds.

Tim Hooey bowhunts turkeys, and though he doesn't always use a blind, he usually does.

"I prefer to use a blind for one reason," Hooey explains. "It's tough to draw on turkeys without being spotted if you're not in a blind. It's really that simple."

Hooey is particular about blinds.

"I want a blind that's black inside, to provide maximum concealment, and I want it to have a lot of windows. It's got to be big enough for two people, because my hunts are filmed and I have to get a cameraman in there with me. I shoot a 40-inch bow, so it has to be big enough for me to hold the bow upright and come to full draw."

Hooey has some specific advice for hunters with new blinds.

"Set up the blind in your backyard and practice shooting from it. Use whatever chair or stool you'll be using, dress in your hunting clothes, simulate the hunting situation as much as possible, and practice in that blind. You need to be sure you can draw your bow comfortably with the setup you have. If not, you can probably make some modifications. If you don't practice from the blind before you go hunting, you're asking for problems."

Though Hooey is talking specifically to bowhunters, a similar point might be made for shotgunners using blinds as well. Practicing shooting in the backyard is probably not practical, but setting up the blind and sitting in it to make sure it's comfortable, that the chair isn't too high or low, that the shooting ports and peepholes are properly positioned, is important. And a little practice setting it up and taking it down can save a lot of frustration in the woods when you find yourself setting up quickly as a gobbler approaches.

Hooey changes his hunting strategy slightly for hunting from blinds. Rarely an aggressive turkey hunter, he is even less so when hunting from a blind, exercising more patience and calling quietly and less frequently.

"The reason I call quietly from the blind is that I can't see around me, or even hear all around me, quite as well. To avoid being silhouetted in a blind, you have to keep most of the windows—at least the ones on one side of the blind—closed.

"Gobblers often sneak in very quietly, and I don't want to start hammering one with cutting and excited calling if he's walking 15 yards behind the blind. Instead, about every 15 minutes I'll purr softly and maybe cluck or yelp quietly. I like slate calls for this sort of calling—maybe it's the higher pitch, but slates seem to work well for me.

"One thing a lot of guys don't think about when they're hunting in a blind is that they really muffle the sound of calls.

Even though I believe in calling quietly, I think it's important to put that call up to an open window so that the sound can carry to the turkeys."

Dick Kirby is another expert who's high on blinds, especially for bowhunters. He, too, is particular about hunting blinds, though he has his own set of particulars.

"A lot of the newer blinds are very lightweight. That's fine if there's no wind, but in the wind these blinds can be worse than useless. Nothing will spook a turkey faster than a blind rattling in the wind. It will spook them every time."

There are two other characteristics that Kirby insists on in his hunting blinds. He wants them to be enclosed 360 degrees, for total concealment, and he wants them to have small openings.

"Hunters should be careful not to silhouette themselves in the blind," cautions Kirby. "In a really good blind, that's about the only way the turkey is going to see you, but you'll get nailed a lot if you do it."

Kirby likes to use decoys with a blind, usually setting them out about 18 to 20 yards away.

"Make sure you have arrow clearance," he cautions. "That may sound obvious, but it's easy to overlook, and I've seen guys aim out the window of a blind and release an arrow right into the fabric."

Although some experts believe that blinds in themselves do not spook turkeys (unless the blinds are rattling in the wind), Kirby is not convinced that turkeys won't sometimes shy away from them.

"I think it's important," he advises, "to dress the blinds up a little with some added concealment. I like to cut some branches, or pick up some sticks, or use vines, leaves, grass, or whatever natural materials are handy to make that blind look a little more natural."

*Blinds with dark interiors allow hunters to see out,
but game can't see in.*

Lovett Williams, ever the scientist, has a minimalist approach to turkey hunting blinds. He rarely if ever uses commercially produced blinds for hunting, pointing out that in his native Florida, where he does most of his turkey hunting, there's plenty of natural concealment.

"I do try to hide," he says. "I plant some grass or some sticks in front of me. Down here we have cabbage palms, and they work very well. One time on a hunt in West Virginia, I was frustrated because I couldn't find a palm frond. Up there, I could have used some camo cloth."

Though he doesn't use blinds in Florida for hunting, he has used them extensively for photographing, recording, and observing turkeys.

"I used to use a tent," he explains. "But in more recent years I've discovered that a simple piece of camo fabric can be very effective. I get that cheap stuff, the stuff that looks like what they covered artillery with in World War II. I just drape it over me, and over the camera, and I've been amazed how well it works.

"With that simple piece of camo draped over me, I can move the camera to get horizontal or vertical shots, and even change the film, and turkeys don't seem to care. They just don't seem to be able to figure out what I am under that cloth.

"I used to worry about being silhouetted, and that sort of thing, but I just don't worry about that anymore.

"In recent years I've been doing a lot of hunting for Gould's turkeys in Mexico. I think I'm going to get me one of those ghillie suits for hunting down there."

Matt Morrett agrees with a growing number of turkey hunters who believe that blinds are all but essential for effectively bowhunting turkeys. He doesn't limit use of blinds strictly to bowhunting, though.

"I think field-edge setups are a great time to use extra concealment, especially in areas where the foliage doesn't lend itself well to blending in."

Though many turkey hunters prefer larger, fully enclosed blinds, Morrett finds that for his turkey hunting something smaller, lighter, and more portable is preferable.

"I like to use a portable blind that just covers me from the front, place it around my position, and use natural cover like a tree or brush for my backdrop."

Our chapter on blinds for turkey hunting would not be complete without some input from Roger Raisch, who was advocating their use long before the comparatively recent explosion of commercially produced hunting blinds.

"I find turkeys seem to be getting wiser as the years go by," observes Raisch, "especially adult gobblers. This is probably due to their having more experiences with man and becoming

*Roger Raisch prefers a cylindrical blind that is tall
enough to allow shooting from a standing position.*

a bit more wary of man-shaped and off-colored objects in their environment."

An avid bowhunter, Raisch has long believed blinds are imperative for those chasing turkeys with a bow. He also recommends them for hunters toting shotguns. Raisch is very particular about the type of blind he uses.

"I almost always use a shield-type camo blind when gun hunting, especially if I'm with another person. This shields out lower bodies and the unavoidable shifting of bodies, and the operation of friction calls, guns, cameras, and the like. Often I'll have to make a last-minute adjustment of the gun or my body to get the proper sight picture before a shot.

"I usually use a very lightweight, 3-foot-tall blind, about 6 to 8 feet long with stakes, made from camouflage material. I prefer the types that have panels with rigid tops and sides, rather than the roll-up types that seem to always be snagged up on something when you want to quickly unroll them. The rigid top makes a good gun rest."

For bowhunting, Roger makes use of a unique blind of his own design. He prefers to shoot standing up, and his blind is shaped like a silo. It's 7 feet tall and 6½ feet in diameter.

Roger believes blinds are less conspicuous if dressed up a little.

"I usually throw some brush up against the blind to further conceal it, and routinely get 10-yard shots at spring gobblers, especially early in the season, before they get wiser."

With any blind, Raisch is a firm believer in decoys, typically using three birds and sometimes as many as seven, including at least one jake or gobbler decoy. When bowhunting, he spends the entire morning in one blind, resisting any temptations to leave the blind or relocate. He keeps a compass and topo map handy, scouting as he hunts by listening carefully and noting the location of gobbling turkeys. He often locates several turkeys in one morning using this approach.

Roger likes to set up blinds at the edge of a woods, or in open areas, in the best strut zones he can find.

"This placement will almost always bring action sometime during a morning's hunt," he asserts.

Roger notes one advantage of hunting from a blind that probably hasn't occurred to most turkey hunters. "What I'm able to do in a blind is to use a lot more different types of calls, simulating a larger flock of turkeys, than when I'm sitting motionless with a gun in my hand and a mouth call in my mouth. In a blind I can select the very best call for the situation at hand, without my motion being seen. I also find that I can imitate the subtle purrs, whines, and clucks with a friction call while inside a blind better than I can with a gun in my hand."

Roger suggests that hunters should reduce the number of decoys they set out, and use extra caution, when hunting in public areas.

He avoids hunting from the same blind day after day, preferring to have several blinds set up and ready for use.

One final bit of advice: Take your camera to the blind.

"This is a way to get excellent photos," he says.

The Ultimate Challenge—Turkeys With a Bow

"Some thangs," a hunting companion of mine from Mississippi once observed, "jus' wasn't meant to be hunted with a bow."

No doubt about it. I've tried pheasant hunting with a bow a few times. I don't think my Brittany, Chester, approved. I've tried squirrel hunting with a bow, too, with limited success. I once arrowed a Canada goose that landed on a pond beside my tree stand, but I'm inclined to think waterfowl aren't ideal candidates for bowhunting, either.

Of course my Mississippi friend was talking about turkeys. He might be right, too. In fact, his words used to ring in my head fairly regularly on many occasions when I made my way out of the woods with bow in hand and nothing over my shoulder. Thing is, we bowhunters who love turkey hunting just can't resist going after turkeys with bows, at least some of the time.

Certainly there are dedicated bowhunters who pursue turkeys exclusively with a bow. My hat is off to them. I worked hard to take my first gobbler with a bow, and for some time after that I struggled on the one hand with the desire to join that elite fraternity of those who consistently kill turkeys with bows, and on the other hand with the desire to have more fun hunting and tag more turkeys. I actually felt guilty at times about choosing my shotgun over my bow. It was ridiculous.

Since then I have found a middle path that has led to peace for me. It's very simple, really. Whenever possible, when I'm on a hunt that allows for taking more than one gobbler, I pursue the first one with my smokepole or my shellshucker. Then, having filled a tag, I pursue gobbler number two with my bow. I typically hunt at least three or four states in a season, and if I'm fortunate enough to bag a few gobblers in the early seasons down South, I may switch exclusively to bowhunting for the later seasons in the North.

Bowhunting without a blind is tough. The challenge is
drawing the bow without being spotted by sharp-eyed turkeys.

When I take my bow to the woods these days, it's with the attitude that I already have my turkey. If I take another with a bow, that's wonderful; if not, I'll savor the excitement of any opportunities, or at least enjoy being outdoors in the springtime. Silly of me, I suppose, to under any circumstances feel pressure to kill a turkey, or experience excessive frustration at failing to, but the approach I've hit on works for me and somehow frees me to enjoy turkey hunting with both shotgun and bow.

All of which is to say that every bowhunter owes it to himself to give bowhunting turkeys a try. It does not have to represent a point of no return. You do not have to chase turkeys exclusively with a bow. It does not have to be the teeth-grinding, hair-pulling, despair-inducing source of frustration that it very nearly became for me. You can still slide the old shotgun out of its case and hunt with it anytime.

And for those who think that pursuing a turkey with a bow is just plain too difficult, I have six words: *portable blinds, mechanical broadheads, string trackers.* The fact is, though it will always represent a real challenge, bowhunting turkeys is not quite the challenge that it was a few years ago because of these developments.

One of the biggest challenges in successfully arrowing a turkey is drawing on it without being detected. Gobblers aren't usually cooperative enough to walk behind a conveniently located tree, or turn away from the hunter in full strut, allowing the bowhunter to draw. New, lightweight, compact blinds that go up and down in seconds nearly eliminate this problem, and without placing too great a limitation on the hunter's mobility.

Another challenge presented by turkeys is that they're relatively small targets, and they have an unfortunate tendency to run or even fly some distance if an arrow doesn't spine them, break a leg, or punch a big hole in their vitals. Big, modern, mechanical broadheads fly like field points for precise shooting, then open up to well over 2 inches to greatly increase the shock

Portable blinds let you draw without being detected.

and the size of the hole they punch. They improve the chance of hitting the vitals and, in the case of a less-than-perfect shot, offer a very good chance of spining the bird or breaking a leg, either of which will anchor it to the spot and ensure recovery.

In the unlikely event that a turkey runs or flies after being struck by a mechanical broadhead, a string tracker will almost guarantee recovery. Gobblers rarely leave a blood trail and can't be tracked for any distance except in snow. String trackers have a minimal effect, if any, on accuracy out to typical turkey bowhunting ranges.

I asked several of our experts who bowhunt turkeys to fill us in on their specific bowhunting setup, as well as to offer some insights into how they go about taking turkeys with bow and arrow.

It might not be readily apparent from watching his television show, but Tim Hooey is a big guy. I felt it might be useful to point this out, because it has a lot to do with his bowhunting setup.

Tim shoots a Mathews Conquest, which he draws comfortably at 75 pounds. He recommends shorter bows to other hunters, but his 30-plus-inch draw length requires something longer. He prefers light, carbon arrows fitted with large mechanical broadheads. With this rig he has a very flat-shooting setup that allows him to use a single sight pin for shots out to 30 yards. He often uses, and advocates use of, a string tracker. Except for the string tracker and the mechanical heads, this is the same setup he uses for deer hunting.

Tim usually, though not always, bowhunts from a blind.

He's a great believer, as are more and more turkey hunters, in mechanical, or open-on-impact, broadheads. "Every turkey I have shot using the mechanical broadhead, I have collected. They are devastating." Tim is sure that the use of mechanical broadheads was a factor in helping him take the Grand Slam with his bow in the spring of 2001.

*Taking a gobbler with a bow is considered by many to be the
supreme turkey hunting challenge.*

Tim has this advice about shot placement, which is critical in turkey hunting.

"The standard advice for turkeys that are in full strut facing away from the hunter is to shoot them right up the vent, and that's good advice. Bowhunters are often told to shoot gobblers where the beard comes out, if the gobblers are facing them, but that's too high. Turkey vitals are lower than that.

"The advice I especially have trouble with is the advice to aim at the wing butt of a turkey standing broadside. You only have to look at a Butterball to see that if you shoot a turkey in the wing butt, you'll miss the vitals and cut through his breast. The place to aim at is about 1 inch behind where the leg meets the body."

This might sound odd, but if you examine the anatomy of the next gobbler you take, you'll see his point. It's important to study a bird closely, though, because seeing exactly where that leg attaches to the body can be difficult at any distance, especially if the gobbler is strutting. The tendency, without knowing the anatomy, will be to shoot too far back.

Tim has one other important bit of advice for those who accept the challenge of hunting turkeys with a bow.

"Mechanical broadheads and string trackers will ensure recovery of most turkeys," he says. "But a bird is going to run or even fly off now and then. Most bowhunters chase them, and that's a mistake. Instead, they should wait half an hour or more. A wounded turkey that isn't being chased will usually stop running and hide pretty quickly, often within 50 or 60 yards. Just watch to see which way he's going, wait a while, then go after him."

Dick Kirby isn't a purist—he has at one time or another hunted turkeys with just about every legal weapon, including handguns. That doesn't mean he's not a serious bowhunter, though, as evidenced by the fact that he has taken the Grand Slam with his bow.

"The kind of bow a hunter uses for turkeys isn't critical," Kirby observes. "What matters is that he has to really believe in his bow. Confidence is what's important.

"I do think quality rests and quality sights are important. I like microadjustable rests. For arrows, I use ACC shafts. They're expensive, but they're worth it. I've often used stoppers behind replaceable-blade broadheads, but more recently I like NAP's mechanical broadheads. Mechanical heads are extremely accurate, and they make a big hole, which is important."

Kirby advocates a reduced draw weight of around 50 to 55 pounds for most turkey chasing bowhunters. A great deal of energy isn't required to take a turkey, and in fact Kirby is among those who believe it's preferable for the arrow to remain in the bird, as opposed to passing through. Further, a low draw weight makes it easier to hold at full draw for extended periods if necessary.

Turkey vitals are a relatively small target, which usually means ranges are reduced as well, at least in comparison to big-game hunting.

"My own personal maximum distance on a turkey is about 35 yards with a bow," says Kirby, "but that's going to vary from one hunter to another. Every hunter needs to determine for himself what his own maximum range is for turkey hunting, but hunters need to keep in mind that the vitals of a gobbler aren't much bigger than a softball, and if they miss the vitals they're unlikely to recover that turkey unless they're lucky enough to spine the bird or break a leg.

"Hunters often think of bowhunting as a close-range kind of deal, which it is, but there is a way to greatly reduce this as a factor, and that is to use decoys. I find I can use decoys to get a

The close range makes bow shots especially challenging.

turkey to go exactly where I want him to. If you put out a couple of hen decoys and a jake decoy, you can be sure the gobbler is going to go straight to that jake every time. Put a jake at 15, 18, 20 yards—whatever range you're most comfortable shooting at—and that's where you'll be shooting."

Kirby has one other bit of advice for bowhunters that he believes is important.

"If you're serious about getting a turkey with a bow," he says slowly, for emphasis, "get a blind."

Bowhunter Roger Raisch currently relies on a Mathews single cam set at 60 pounds for his turkey hunting. He likes short bows for hunting from blinds.

"I use a scope," says Roger, "like the 3D professionals use, with no magnifying lens." Roger has found that lenses tend to fog up, especially in the confines of an enclosed blind. "I like either a single pin or open crosshairs inside the scope, set at 20 yards. If a shot presents itself closer than that, I'm slightly lower."

A confirmed finger shooter, he admits he would probably shoot more accurately with a release aid, but is accustomed to finger shooting and confident in his proficiency. He does limit his range to 20 yards.

"I place orange surveyor's tape at 20 yards all around my blind, and don't shoot unless a turkey is 20 yards or closer. Better shots than me could probably stretch that range to 30 yards, but I don't have the condidence to shoot accurately beyond 20, especially dragging a string tracker.

"My most difficult shot, however, is the 5-yard shot. I've shot many holes in my blinds below the shooting window, because the bird was too close. I like those 10-yard shots."

Roger swears by string trackers, but goes one step better.

"My nearly foolproof setup," he explains, "is a Game Tracker

The TrackMaster never fails when it comes to finding downed turkeys—assuming the arrow stays in the bird.

string tracker, shooting 30-pound line, along with an electronic arrow tracking system. The electronic TrackMaster system consists of a tiny transmitter that fits inside the arrow shaft. When the arrow is shot, the transmitter is automatically activated. A directional receiver is used to track the arrow. I always find my arrow, generally in a very dead turkey, but often hundreds of yards away. Without these systems, many of my turkeys would not have been recovered. Over the years, I have lost very few turkeys with this setup."

The rest of Roger's setup consists of aluminum arrows, a flipper-style rest, and wide-cutting broadheads. "The wider the better," asserts Roger.

"I have bagged several gobblers with the expanding mechanical broadheads, but I don't use them because I usually have a string tracker attached to the arrow. The string from the

Mechanical broadheads, closed and opened.

tracker tends to pull an arrow with an expanding head out of the bird, especially if there's a poor hit."

Roger always uses a blind when bowhunting, along with decoys, and is disciplined about staying in the same blind, at the same location, all morning. He relies on scouting to locate good strut zones, and is convinced that this strategy is the most effective way to bowhunt turkeys.

Dedicated bowhunter Steve Puppe is very meticulous—and very specific—about his bowhunting setup for turkeys.

"I use a Mathews SQ2 bow because it's short, compact, and easy to maneuver while on the ground, Truglo fiber-optic sights, and T.R.U. Ball Tornado release. I shoot NAP Gobbler Getters for turkeys, which have a blunt tip and expanding blades."

Puppe, like Dick Kirby, prefers that the arrow stay in the bird.

"The blunt tip helps prevent a pass-through. I like the arrow to stay in the bird if it doesn't take him down instantly. I don't use a string tracker as generally turkeys will go only a short distance with this broadhead, which has a full 2½-inch cut."

Puppe lets the local environment determine whether or not he uses a blind.

"I use a blind about 50 percent of the time," he says, "depending on the terrain and the subspecies I'm hunting. Some areas require a blind because of lack of cover, and a blind helps to conceal movement.

"As far as my hunting strategies go when bowhunting, they differ little from gun hunting other than the fact that I have to be more patient when bowhunting, and do less running and gunning."

An excellent shot, Puppe limits his range to less than 30 yards when bowhunting turkeys.

"Turkey hunting with a bow? Yes, I hunt 'em with a bow sometimes. It's hard." So says Larry Norton, with a chuckle.

"I recommend a blind and decoys. We can't use decoys in Alabama, which makes it even harder. I'd say decoys are almost a must for bowhunters, if you can use them. Blinds should be fully enclosed and dark inside.

"My bowhunting setup is almost the same as the setup I use for deer," Larry continues, "except for two things. First, I drop the draw weight down as low as it will go on my bow, which is usually 55 or 60 pounds in my case. Also, I use expandable broadheads. I don't like them for deer hunting, but they're ideal for turkey hunting."

Larry agrees fully with Tim Hooey about the location of a turkey's vitals, which he insists are not only farther back, but also lower than most hunters realize. He has this advice for arrow placement on turkeys that are facing the hunter.

"A lot of guys try to shoot where the beard comes out, but that's too high. It's a small target, for one thing, with very little

Useful for any turkey hunter, decoys offer special advantage for bowhunters, who need close shots at unwary gobblers.

margin for error. But a turkey's vitals aren't that high anyway. The best spot to aim is farther down, where the breast flattens out, almost between the thighs. I mean where the knob is—you know that little spot that gets worn from riding hens? That's the spot."

8

Optics for Turkey Hunters

My optometrist tells me that my vision, when wearing the contact lenses she has prescribed to correct astigmatism, is a perfect 20–20. Turkey hunting tells me that 20–20 is not good enough.

Like many experienced turkey hunters, I enjoy taking youngsters out hunting. It's often a humbling experience. Yes, they fidget, they talk, and they grow impatient, but that's not the humbling part. The humbling part is that they see turkeys before I do, they see turkeys I never see, and with a little education they can tell a gobbler from a jake before I'm certain that black spot way out in the meadow isn't a crow. Twenty-twenty or not, my vision just isn't what it used to be.

Truth is, though, the best human vision is no match for that of a turkey. Add to their keen eyes the facts that their peripheral vision is much wider than ours (they can all but see behind themselves), they are extremely quick to detect motion, they are perpetually wary, their reaction time is astonishing, and they have very little if any of the curiosity that will sometimes prompt pronghorns, deer, or other game to stop and stare at, or even approach, that camo-clad object in the shadows they can't quite make out. This spring thousands of turkey hunters will peek around a bend in a logging road, or lean out from behind a hedge to scan a meadow, and see one or more turkeys. And in almost every case, unless the distance is great, the turkeys will be looking right back at them, prepared to run or fly long before the gun gets to the shoulder—that is, if they aren't already running or flying.

It is possible to improve the odds a little. Remaining motionless when seated or standing is important. Good camo helps. And while stalking gobblers is a low-percentage tactic and not recommended for safety reasons, it is possible for skilled stalkers who move slowly and carefully, sticking to the shadows and taking full advantage of terrain and cover, to close the distance on turkeys without being detected. More to the point, good binoculars, properly used, can give hunters an additional edge. The best way to spot turkeys before they spot you is to see them at a distance. Binoculars can help you do this, as well as to distinguish gobblers from jakes and hens. And even at closer ranges, the hunter who is well concealed and sitting still can sometimes use binoculars to spot a turkey in a heavily shaded area, or to detect movement through a screen of vegetation.

Hunting effectiveness isn't the only reason to carry binoculars afield. Many turkey hunters (probably most) like to hunt mushrooms, identify songbirds, or watch deer and other wildlife in the turkey woods, and binoculars are helpful, if not essential, for all these things. No, using binoculars this way isn't improving your turkey hunting, but it does enhance your time outdoors.

Binoculars aren't the only optical devices that are useful for turkey hunters, and for some they aren't even the most impor-

*Binoculars allow hunters to spot and observe
turkeys from a discreet distance.*

tant. Any hunters approaching middle age and discovering a need for reading glasses or bifocals are quite likely to have difficulty focusing on a shotgun bead, not to mention iron sights. The easy answer for these hunters is a good scope, red-dot, or holographic sighting device. The combination of a relatively small target and a tight pattern demands precise shooting, and scopes, along with the other devices mentioned, are tailor-made for this kind of shooting. Good turkey hunting scopes are low powered, often 1.5 or 2X, to admit plenty of light and offer a wide field of view for quick target acquisition. One caveat applies here, though—it's easy when looking through even a low-powered scope to underestimate range. One fix for this is to observe the turkey outside the scope until he's in range. Some hunters take advantage of peep-through-type scope mounts, raising their eye to the scope at the last moment before shooting.

Another option is a good rangefinder. Laser rangefinders such as those marketed by Nikon, Bushnell, and Leica are among the optical accessories that increasing numbers of turkey hunters won't leave home without. All are accurate to within a yard or so at turkey hunting ranges. By quickly ranging on a few landmarks around any setup, a hunter can greatly reduce range estimation errors as a factor in turkey hunting, and can hunt with the confidence inspired by knowing exactly when that strutting tom is in range.

Perhaps the best case to be made for optics, though, is the fact that most—though not all—of our experts believe firmly in them.

Eddie Salter relies on his binoculars primarily as a scouting tool. From roads, ridgetops, or field edges, he can scan large areas quickly, and from a distance that won't alert birds. Distinguishing gobblers from hens, let alone from jakes, isn't always a cinch at several hundred yards, especially on a cloudy day, or if

Laser rangefinders: Don't leave home without them!
A growing number of turkey hunters consider laser
rangefinders worthwhile investments.

the birds are obscured by trees or brush, or moving quickly through the field of view. Binoculars make the difference.

"These days," according to Salter, "some turkey hunters are getting more selective. They hunt for trophy gobblers the way some deer hunters hunt for big bucks. They're not interested in just any gobbler—they're waiting for a big longbeard with good spurs. At 75 yards with my Swarovski, I can see a gobbler's spurs."

For a rangefinder, Salter tends to rely on his own judgment, based on years of experience in the turkey woods.

"I tell hunters to think of a football field," Salter explains. "Pick out some landmarks and imagine 5 yards, 10 yards, and so on, out to your maximum shotgun range."

Salter has at times used scoped shotguns, and touts the ability of some scopes to serve as good rangefinders. Hunters don't necessarily have to know exactly how far away a given turkey might be, he points out. What they really need to know is whether or not the bird is in range.

"A diamond reticle can work well as a rangefinder. The last one I used was perfect for that. If the gobbler was all inside the diamond, he was out of range. When he was too big to fit inside that diamond, he was in range and I knew I could shoot and make a clean kill."

John McDaniel has an interesting take on optics for turkey hunters, though his use of them is limited. Many experts recommend that turkey hunters use laser rangefinders to determine the range to several landmarks when first setting up in a spot. McDaniel doesn't use them in quite that way.

"I use a laser rangefinder," John told me in a recent conversation, "but I don't really find them practical in hunting situations. I have found them very useful, though, for sharpening my range estimating abilities. I estimate the distance to something, then check it with my rangefinder."

McDaniel finds little use for binoculars in the mountainous, heavily forested areas where he spends much of his time turkey hunting, nor does he scope his shotgun. He points out that he has never felt handicapped by the lack of a scope, but his main reason for not using one is that he wants to be able to take turkeys on the wing and feels—correctly, no doubt—that a scope would hinder this ability. In fact, McDaniel is a meticulous record keeper, and his logs reveal that fully 22 percent of the turkeys he has taken were taken on the wing.

I should explain that McDaniel does a lot of fall turkey hunting, often with dogs, and most of the turkeys he has taken on the wing were fall turkeys. Even for spring turkeys, though, McDaniel wants to be fully prepared for the rare wounded gobbler that takes to the air or regains its feet and needs a quick finishing shot.

It's a good point, and one that hunters who, like myself, have been pondering the use of scopes on their shotguns should keep in mind. The need for a follow-up shot should be a rare occurrence, but sooner or later every turkey hunter is going to experience it. Turkeys are virtually untrackable. Wounded ones that fly or run off are difficult to find, so it's important to anchor them to the spot. One possible compromise: a peep-through-type scope mount that gives hunters the option of using the scope or looking down the barrel.

Peter Fiduccia is a great believer in quality optics of all kinds, and relies heavily on his Leica rangefinder and Leupold binoculars and scopes.

"I wouldn't hunt without them," asserts Fiduccia. "I think optics are a crucial piece of turkey hunting equipment, and not only for scouting but for hunting as well."

Most experts make some use of binoculars, and increasing numbers are taking advantage of laser rangefinders. Scopes have a smaller niche, but Peter touts them highly.

"Scopes will put more birds in the freezer," he insists. "A good scope can make the difference between success and failure."

Like Eddie Salter, Fiduccia points out the ability of binoculars to distinguish the quality of a given gobbler. While to most turkey hunters (and I put myself in this category), any mature gobbler is a trophy, growing numbers of hunters are inevitably becoming more selective as they achieve consistent success. To these hunters, a gobbler is not just a gobbler—they want a true longbeard, or a bird with impressive spurs. I'm aware of some hunters, usually in heavily agricultural areas where turkeys often achieve weights of 22 pounds or more, who pay attention not only to the length of the beard and the spurs, but also to the size of the turkey. Clearly, high-quality binoculars are essential tools for selective turkey hunters.

Finally, Fiduccia cautions hunters not to assume that the use of a scope means they don't have to pattern their shotguns.

"Scopes aid in making sure the pellets are going to hit where you aim, but they don't improve the pattern. Hunters still need to pattern their shotguns."

Having guided a number of turkey hunters, and noticed that a surprisingly high percentage of both new and experienced hunters alike have never patterned their guns, I have to second that motion.

I asked Paul Butski about optics for turkey hunting.
"Don't use 'em," he said.

Larry Norton, on the other hand, is a firm believer in optics of all sorts. He uses binoculars, for instance, for the usual purpose of spotting turkeys and distinguishing gobblers from jakes and hens at a distance, but he also once taught me a particularly useful trick for hunting turkeys in fields.

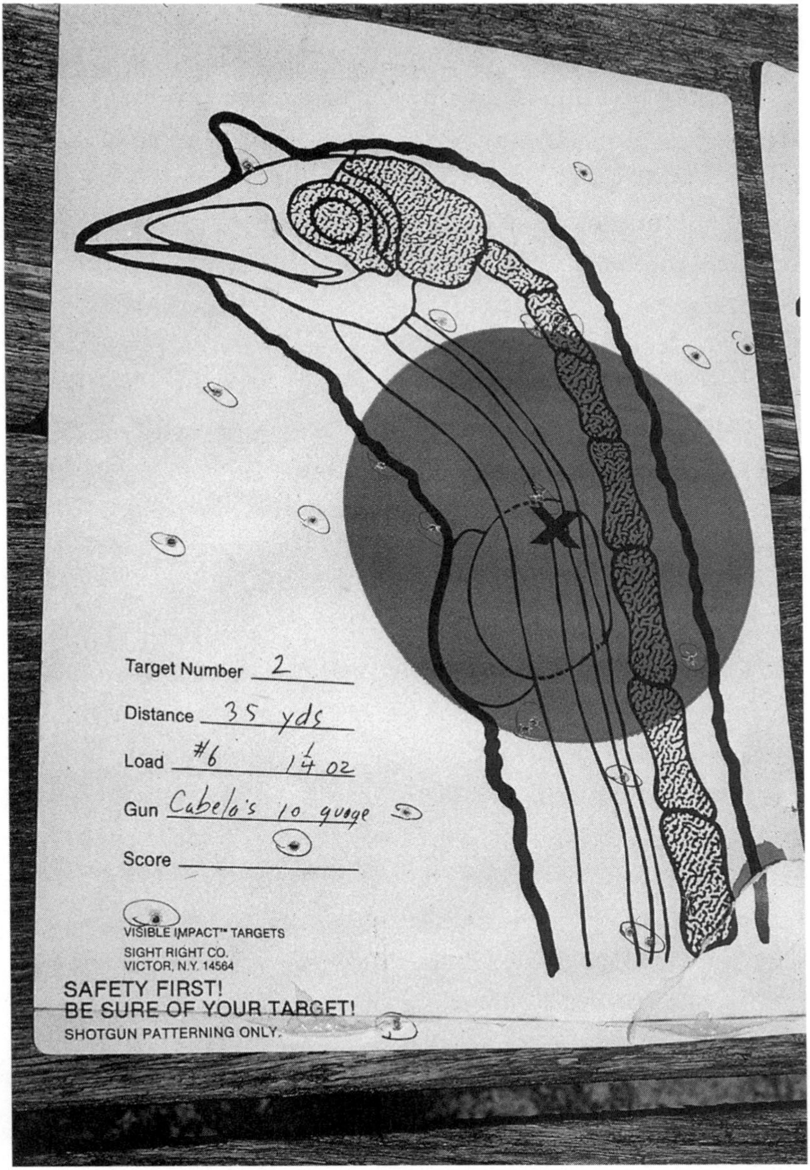

Every hunter should pattern his shotgun on a turkey target.

Approaching a field to look for turkeys is a tricky business—if you don't do it very carefully, the wary birds will probably spot you at the same moment you spot them, if not before. Instead of peeping around the edge of a field, or sneaking in on a logging road, Larry tries to approach them from the concealment of thick foliage. Then he'll use the binoculars to look through the foliage. All it takes is a slightly thin spot, and the binoculars will throw the foliage out of focus, enabling the hunter to in effect look right through it.

Laser rangefinders are another item Larry values highly.

"Most hunters who miss turkeys are just shooting at them too far away. They get excited, they underestimate the range of that big gobbler in full strut, and they shoot too soon. With a laser rangefinder, you just take a quick reading on a few rocks or stumps when you set up, and when that turkey comes in you know right away when he's in range."

More recently, he's discovered red-dot sights for his scope.

"A friend of mine showed me his Tasco red-dot scope a few years ago, and I went out and got one. They're great. You put the dot on the turkey's head and that's where the pattern will go. I've missed turkeys before when shooting from awkward positions, like way around to the right. You cant the gun a little bit, or you don't get your head down against the stock, and you'll miss. With these scopes, that's not an issue. Shoot left-handed, whatever, it doesn't matter. If the scope is on the turkey's head, you kill the turkey."

Larry is especially high on these scopes for kids. He bought his daughter one and is convinced it helped her kill her first gobbler.

Can they slow down target acquisition?

"No," Larry says emphatically. "You can wingshoot with these scopes. In fact," he points out, "some dove hunters use them. They have no magnification. You can also use them with peep-through scope mounts, if you want to, but I'm not sure there's a need for that."

It seems that the range of opinions is wider on this topic than on any other, with some experts swearing by optics, while others feel they're unimportant or even in the way. The opinions above are representative of similar conversations I had with others. Perhaps the fairest thing that can be said about optics for turkey hunters is that they're a tool, much like a certain locator call, a decoy, or a blind. Sometimes the call, the decoy, or the blind makes a difference, and sometimes it's not a factor. Is the decoy worth carrying if it *sometimes* makes a difference? That's going to depend to a large extent on just how often the hunter perceives it to make a difference, which will depend to some extent on where he hunts, how he hunts, and what kind of decoy it is.

There are a couple of situations in which telescopic sights can make a clear and dramatic difference. One, as previously

Author with a bow-killed turkey. Scouting with binoculars
before the season helped him find the perfect set-up spot.

mentioned, is when age or other conditions make it impossible for a hunter to clearly see the bead or the iron sights on a shotgun. A scope is often the simple solution to this problem.

The other situation applies to hunters who frequently miss turkeys, usually because of nervousness or excitement. They don't get their cheek firmly against the stock in many cases, or they just point the gun and shoot it without aiming. Often these are youngsters or people who are simply new to the sport. Whatever their circumstances, I'm not in the least bit inclined to ridicule them—I even envy them. Turkey hunting is an exciting sport, and when I no longer get excited as a longbeard approaches, I'll stop getting out of bed at 4 A.M. and hang my gun up. The fellows who get buck fever apparently find it even more exciting than I do.

A scope can help a lot, and often cures the problem. The hunter is forced to mount the gun properly to see clearly through the scope, and the need to put the crosshairs on the target improves the aim and solves the problem of simply looking over the barrel and shooting. And, as Larry Norton points out, some of the new holographic or red-dot type scopes eliminate even the need for proper shooting form.

Kate Fiduccia with gobbler she took with shotgun without a scope.

9

Calling Secrets

A quick glance through the spring issue of any good hunting supply catalog reveals clearly that the entrepreneurial spirit is alive and well in the USA. Modern hunters can gaze at page after page of an amazing array of gadgets, gizmos, and devices designed to reproduce the sounds of a turkey. There are box calls, tube calls, diaphragm calls, wingbone calls, slate calls, scratch boxes—and those are just the basics! That doesn't include newfangled devices such as pump calls, or those funny-looking round calls that appear to have dials and buttons sticking out of them. (What *are* those things, anyway?) It also doesn't include new calls designed to imitate the sounds of a gobbler spitting and drumming, flying down from the roost, or even rubbing his feathers against tree bark. And then there's the whole category of locator calls. Is this a great country, or what?

It has become fashionable among turkey hunters to de-emphasize the importance of calling skills, and to assert that knowledge and woodsmanship is far more important. Few experienced hunters, including champion callers such as Larry Norton and Eddie Salter, will deny this assertion, but Eddie Salter once related to me a story that helps illustrate the role calling plays in turkey hunting.

It seems a champion caller of his acquaintance was guiding an outdoor writer on a spring turkey hunt. The outdoor writer was particularly insistent about the relative unimportance of calling as a factor in successful turkey hunting. The champion caller was inclined to agree that calling probably wasn't the single most important factor in turkey hunting, but over time the writer's constant downplaying of the importance of calling skills began to grate on the guide's nerves, who had, after all, devoted no small amount of time to perfecting his technique.

On the first morning of the hunt, the guide led the writer through a mature, open woods to the edge of a hillside meadow. As sunrise approached and the woods began coming to life, they were greeted by a booming gobble from a tom somewhere on the other side of the meadow.

"Well, I've led you to your gobbler," said the guide. "Now go get him with your woodsmanship."

The guide's point, of course, was that no matter how important other factors may be in bagging a turkey, it's almost always calling that brings him into shotgun range.

Yes, we could hunt turkeys without calling them. We could bait them, for instance, or we could shoot them with rifles from 200 yards away. Both are legal in some places, and I'm not inclined to sit in judgment on fellow hunters who hunt turkeys this way and who are abiding by game laws and otherwise hunting ethically, but this just isn't turkey hunting as most hunters wish to experience it.

It's also true that turkeys can be simply ambushed. This is a tactic to which I have no objections; I have in fact used it successfully on several occasions. I don't object to it because,

Author calling to a distant gobbler with a slate call.

frankly, it's usually a more challenging way to bag a gobbler than is calling one in.

There is a mystique surrounding not only calling turkeys, but the calls themselves as well. Some calls have more mystique than others. There's very little mystique around diaphragm mouth calls, for instance. I've seen some very good tube calls made with film canisters, but there's little mystique surrounding those, either. A good box call has it, though, as do some slate calls, wingbone calls, and others. I suppose there's no explaining *mystique,* or it wouldn't be, well, mystique. But in the case of turkey calls, it seems to have something to do with the materials from which they are made. Natural materials, such as wood, bone, or ivory, have it; calls made largely of plastic, fiberglass, or aluminum don't have it.

I have an unfortunate tendency to leave calls in the woods, often after I've bagged a gobbler. Years ago I enjoyed a memorable hunt for Osceolas in the Everglades. A friend I made on that hunt gave me a Tom Gaskins scratch box. I liked the little call, and used it over the years to call in a number of turkeys. Then, on a hunt in Indiana, I bagged a big tom, slung it over my shoulder, and hiked off through the woods, leaving my treasured little scratch box in the leaves by the oak tree I had sat against. I discovered it missing when I unpacked at home. I got in my car, drove 70 or 80 miles back across the state line into Indiana, hiked back to the spot, and used my flashlight to find the call.

Then I left it on the edge of a south-central Ohio meadow, outside the blind from which I had called a strutting tom to within 12 yards before putting an arrow through his chest. This time I didn't miss the call immediately, and when I did I wasn't sure where I'd left it. I found it the next spring, when I returned to set up a blind in the same spot. Rodents had gnawed on it, and it was weathered by the elements, but when I chalked it up and stroked it, it sounded sweeter than ever. I still have it, and still use it.

I have an Eddie Salter box call, too, that I've used for many years. I have long intended to have Eddie sign it for me, but it always seems that no one has a pen handy, or the pen won't write, or I don't have it with me when I see him, or I just plain forget about it in the excitement of a hunting camp.

I talked to Eddie Salter recently about calling and its role in turkey hunting. Eddie is among the world-champion turkey callers who readily concede that woodsmanship skills are more important than calling skills when it comes to bagging a gobbler.

You might suppose that Eddie's aggressive hunting style would lend itself to aggressive calling, and often it does. Eddie is a great believer in putting emotion into calling. He believes the turkeys are more likely to respond, and more likely to get fired up after responding, if the caller conveys excitement in his calls. He regularly admonishes hunters to "put some life" into their calling.

One of his favorite calls, in fact, is one he calls a "feeling" call. It consists of three or four quick cuts, followed by seven or eight old hen yelps. Usually the call starts off low-key, then becomes louder in volume, faster, and higher pitched to convey emotion.

Salter doesn't always call aggressively. He tends to start with aggressive calling, especially early in the season, then backs off on the volume and excitement level as the season progresses. As a general rule, he tries to let the gobblers dictate the calling style—what many turkey hunters refer to as taking a gobbler's temperature.

"If I yelp and that gobbler starts cutting me off as I call, he's telling me he wants to ride home in my truck. I'll do a lot of loud yelping and cutting to that bird. If the bird waits a while before gobbling back at my calls, I figure he's already heard all the popular brands of turkey calls. I'll call that turkey much less aggressively. In some cases I might call once or twice, then quit."

Eddie likes to talk about locator calls.

"When people talk about calling, they don't give a lot of attention to locator calls," he says. "That's a mistake. Before you need a turkey call, you need to locate the turkey."

Eddie advises hunters to practice using their locator calls in order to get more volume out of them. Volume is important in locating turkeys; not only will it reach out to cover more ground, but even close-in birds are more likely to be shocked into gobbling if the volume is loud.

Traditional owl and crow calls are good locators, but they don't always work. Eddie likes to have another type of locator, such as a hawk or a pileated woodpecker call, for mornings on which the owls and crows seem to be sounding off nonstop, or to try when the owl and crow calls simply don't get responses.

"These kinds of locators don't always work," he admits, "but they're worth trying first. After I've tried them a few times, I'll reach for a turkey call and use loud cutting as a locator."

Larry Norton is another aggressive southern turkey hunter, and his calling style reflects it. He disagrees with many other

When a gobbler gets within range, many hunters
stop calling. Larry Norton does just the opposite.

experts on one aspect of calling: calling to birds that are in close.

"Most hunters will tell you that when the gobbler gets close, stop calling. When I get a gobbler coming in, I want him to keep coming in. I don't want to take a chance that a hen will come along and wander off with him, or that he'll just plain lose interest. I don't stop calling until I pull the trigger, or the hunter I'm guiding does."

Like any good turkey hunter, though, Norton will adjust his tactics to suit the situation. I encountered one such situation on a hunt with Norton at Alabama's famous Bent Creek Lodge, where he guides. Norton worked a seemingly fired-up gobbler expertly, but just before he came within sight, he began to fade. We carefully moved closer and set up again, and once again the gobbler approached, gobbling lustily, only to reverse his course and move away just before we expected to see him.

We huddled to talk strategy.

"The gobbler is henned up," he explained.

I guess I looked skeptical

"C'mon, I'll show you. Listen closely as he approaches and you'll hear them."

Once again we relocated and began working the bird in, but this time, as he got close, I could hear the faint but insistent yelping and clucking of hens in the background before he faded. It seemed he wanted a date with Larry's call, but was reluctant to get too far away from his harem. Whenever he started to wander out of sight, they threatened to leave and he went home.

We left with plans to return later, but heavy rain spoiled our plans. At the lodge, I asked Larry what his strategy would have been.

"A lot of hunters talk about challenging the dominant hen. The idea is that if she gets mad and wants to fight, she'll come to the call and bring the gobbler with her. But in my experience, if you challenge the dominant hen she is far more often than not going to go the other way, and the gobbler will follow her.

"The best approach I've found is to slip in as close as you can get, then begin calling very quietly and calmly. Sometimes I think the hen believes the caller is part of the flock, and moves that way. But whatever the reason, a little quiet calling seems to have a better chance in this situation than does loud cutting and other aggressive calls that challenge the hen."

He agrees with Eddie Salter about the importance of locator calls.

"You have to locate a turkey before you can do anything else. The hunter who locates more turkeys gets to work more turkeys, and in the long run will kill more turkeys. It's as simple as that."

Norton locates them in part by covering a lot of ground, but he's a great believer in locator calls. He relies mostly on crow calls, but also uses owl and coyote calls, hawk calls, and occasionally even a duck call. He'll resort to hen yelps when necessary, but always tries the locator calls first.

"If you get him to yelp at a locator, you can take your time and figure him out, maybe find out whether he has hens with him or not. If he does have hens and you've started with a hen yelp, there's a very good chance that while you're finding a place to set up, that hen is leading him off to the next county somewhere. If he doesn't have hens, he could be headed your way in a hurry and catch you unprepared in a bad spot."

After locating a bird on the roost, Larry likes to get within 100 yards of him if terrain or foliage permits. On the ground, he tends to keep his distance.

"If I get a gobble at 300 yards, I might just sit down right there on the spot and wait to see what he's doing. A lot of guys bump birds trying to close in on them. After I figure out what the gobbler is doing, I might move toward him carefully, about

50 yards at a time. I often move at an angle, instead of going straight to him, and I think it's a mistake to hurry toward him in that situation.

"I also think it's a mistake to call while you're moving toward a gobbler. I don't want him to think the hen—me—is coming to him. If he thinks that, he's liable to just do what gobblers usually do, and stay right where he is waiting for that hen."

Larry recommends practice, practice, and more practice when it comes to turkey calling.

"I think competitive turkey calling helped me be a better turkey caller," he muses.

"This happened to me a lot when I first started turkey hunting, and I think it happens to a lot of inexperienced turkey hunters. They may call reasonably well, but they don't have a lot of confidence in their calling. They're afraid to call when that bird hangs up just out of range and is looking right at them. They're afraid they'll mess up and spook the bird. A little purr or cluck might be all that's needed to bring him in, but they don't do it and miss the opportunity. Or they try the call, and because they're nervous and lack confidence in their calling, they *do* mess up and spook the turkey. That lack of confidence is why I started calling competitively, and I think it helped my turkey hunting a lot."

Tim Hooey is humble about his calling skills, but perhaps that's because he spends so much time hunting with world-champion callers. In fact, Hooey is an excellent caller who never stops practicing his techniques. He learns a great deal from the competitive callers he hunts with, but his interest is not focused on what impresses calling judges, but on what fools turkeys. And on this subject he has over the years developed some definite opinions of his own.

"Calling well is important," Hooey insists, "especially when hunting pressured birds. I think sometimes we hesitate to say that because we don't want to discourage people from coming into the sport. And the fact is that just about anybody can call in a gobbler at times. There are situations, though, in which calling skills make a difference. I want to sound as much like a turkey as I can, and I never quit practicing, I'm never satisfied with my calling. Turkey hunters should call as well as they can."

Hooey makes no apologies for his comparatively laid-back calling style.

"There are situations in which I will call aggressively, but my inclination is to keep it low-key. My calling rarely says to a gobbler, 'Hey, get your butt over here, now!' It's more of a quiet, 'Here I am, honey.' Sometimes I don't call back to a gobbler at all."

Hooey prefers to feel that he isn't prompting gobbles.

"You cutt and a gobbler sounds off 200 yards away. Maybe he is interested, maybe it was just a courtesy gobble. You jerked a gobble out of him. Even if he continues to gobble in response to your excited cutting, he may not be coming your way. But if I yelp quietly and he gobbles immediately, that turkey can be killed."

In a similar vein, Hooey rarely uses locator calls.

"I want the turkey to tell *me* when he's ready to die. The bird that's sounding off a lot, gobbling regularly on his own, without prompting, is the one I want to go after."

This is one situation, by the way, in which Hooey will call aggressively. Another is whenever he's hunting Merriam's turkeys.

"Merriam's are the most vocal birds, and it just seems to me you have to really hammer them. I call aggressively to Merriam's."

When I asked him in a recent conversation if he had a favorite call, he became very animated.

"Yes, I do. I have one call that I love to do. It's two clucks that roll immediately into two falling-off yelps . . . they like that. I heard a hen do it once, and several gobblers in the area went nuts, so I added it to my arsenal of calls."

Hooey not only is knowledgeable about turkey calling but has over the years amassed considerable knowledge about turkey calls as well.

"A lot of guys are careless with their mouth calls," he says. "They're really only prime for song long before they wear out, and they'll wear out a lot faster if you don't take care of them. They should be kept out of the light as much as possible, because light breaks them down. The freezer is a good place to keep them. They need to be cleaned with mouthwash now and then, too.

"Turkey hunters shouldn't be afraid to play around with their calls. When it comes to mouth calls, for instance, everyone's palate is different, and what sounds good for one guy might not work for another. Try a lot of different shapes, styles, and sizes to get the best one for you. And don't hesitate to modify them, either. Cut a slit in one, a notch in another. Sometimes a mediocre call becomes a great one when a hunter cuts a slit in it."

Similarly, Hooey advises hunters to experiment with different pegs on their slate calls.

"Lots of times the peg, or striker, is more important to the sound than is the slate itself. Try different ones until you find the one that's perfect for a given slate. For my own part, I think hard wooden strikers are superior to other types."

As a final tip, Hooey advises hunters, especially inexperienced hunters who lack confidence in their calling, to avoid calling to gobblers when they're close in.

"Any turkey call sounds more authentic at a distance than at close range. When I get a bird in very close, I call very little if at all. Why risk spooking him now? What does work very well, if you can get away with the movement, is to reach behind your back carefully and scratch in the leaves. It's easy to do, but you have to know how turkeys scratch. They always scratch once with one foot, then scratch twice quickly with the other foot. Sort of a 'scratch, scratch-scratch.'"

Perhaps none of the responses to my questions about calling skills surprised me more than those of Lovett Williams. The author of *The Voice and Vocabulary of the Wild Turkey*, Williams has spent countless hours recording the sounds of turkeys, cataloging them, and writing about them. More than a few turkey hunters have learned to call turkeys by listening to the popular series of recordings he produced.

"I de-emphasize the importance of calling skills to people who want to call turkeys," he explains. "Many of the old-timers could kill turkeys regularly without calling at all. I killed turkeys without a call for four or five years, before I learned to call on my own. And my own favorite turkey hunting now is in the fall, when I spend most of my time reading sign.

"I believe a guy with a few basic skills can go into the woods in the spring and call in a gobbler. That's the way most people want to hunt turkeys these days, and I write for those hunters."

If Lovett's relative lack of emphasis on calling skills was surprising, his approach to calling is perfectly consistent with his skeptical, scientific attitude.

"I think more turkey hunters need to understand that in the spring, you are simply trying to make a gobbler think that there are turkeys where you are. That's all you do. Which calls you make doesn't matter."

In Lovett's experience, turkeys are social creatures, and a gobbler may approach to investigate the source of anything that sounds like another turkey. End of story.

"Mostly I yelp," he says. "I will vary that from time to time, but more for myself, so I don't get bored, than for the turkeys. I play around with a wingbone call a lot, and 90 percent of my calling is simple, loud yelping. When a turkey gets within 150 yards or so, I'll go to short yelps, just loud enough to be heard."

Williams doesn't reduce the volume of his calls because he fears that volume in itself spooks turkeys, though. He's convinced it doesn't.

"At a distance, loud calls can sound very authentic," he explains. "But up close, a call sounds more like a turkey if it's not too loud. If you listen to a loud call up close, sometimes you can hear the mechanism of the call. It just doesn't sound as much like a real turkey."

Matt Morrett has no qualms about attributing importance to calling.

"For years I've heard that calling is less than 10 percent of the game," he asserts. "I strongly disagree with this statement. I think that trying to your best ability to imitate real turkey sounds and rhythm, and knowing when and how to call, is well over 90 percent of successfully, year after year, bringing longbeards into range.

"My go-to call in any situation is hen yelping. I know that's boring, but with yelping I can add excitement to fire a gobbler up, or I can soften it down to keep him guessing."

Dick Kirby attributes 30 to 40 percent of turkey hunting success to calling, 60 or 70 percent, he feels, is due to woodsmanship and knowledge of turkeys.

"It all has to come together," insists Kirby. "You've got to really screw up badly to spook a turkey with a call. At the same time, confidence is very important in turkey hunting, and good calling skills will really boost a hunter's confidence."

Kirby relies heavily on boat paddle box calls, especially for locating turkeys, and on slate calls. Together, he feels these are the most realistic-sounding calls in the turkey woods. Mouth calls do have the advantage of diversity, he points out. He also believes there are situations in which the boat paddle call is just too loud.

"Think of turkey hunting as a chess game," he suggests. "I'm looking for a gobbler, and I find him. Now I've gotta turn that around, so he's looking for me. Many hunters just aren't patient enough in playing that game.

"You're working a gobbler, and when he shuts up, you worry. What's he doing? Is he coming this way? Is he hung up? Sneaking off?

"Remember that this works both ways. When *you* shut up, *he* worries. When you get *him* worrying about where *you* went, he's a dead bird."

The Perfect Setup

It's a basic question, but an important one. Where should you set up on a gobbling turkey—or, for that matter, start blind calling when the gobblers have lockjaw? This decision can often be the most important one a turkey hunter will make.

I can still remember hiking over the low, rolling hills of south-central Ohio in a thick, second-growth area on one of my first turkey hunts. I'd been out scouting a few times with experienced hunters, had heard a few birds gobble, and had even observed a friend working a gobbler expertly with a box call until a sudden cloudburst cut the conversation short. Now I was hunting alone, working my way up the hill at first light, more intent on finding my way in unfamiliar country than on listening for turkeys. The gobbler probably sounded off three or four times before I noticed it. Wait, is that a gobbler? Yes!

I was excited just to be there, in the woods in possession of a turkey tag and a loaded shotgun, with a gobbler sounding off from somewhere not too far away. I was content for half a minute or so to just stand there and enjoy the sensation.

Perfect concealment helped this hunter take a nice Merriam's gobbler.

Now what? I didn't have a clue. Well, that's not quite right, I had a clue, if only a clue. I was supposed to sit against a tree and yelp on the box call. The turkey would gobble back, I would yelp again, and soon a long-bearded gobbler would be in sight, strutting and drumming his way into shotgun range. But where to sit? Should I try to get closer? How close? Should I get to the top of the hill, or stay below the crest? It was too thick where I stood, but was it too open over there?

Many years and quite a few gobblers later, I still can't answer these questions with confidence. Oh, I can make some generalizations about selecting a good, wide tree to sit against for the sake of safety, about not sitting where vision or movement will be obstructed, about sitting with your left shoulder pointed in the general direction from which you expect the gobbler to come. To this I might add that a hunter is much less visible in the shade than in the sun. Then there's the factor of comfort. If you can't sit comfortably, you won't be able to sit still. Movement, more than anything else, is what betrays hunters to sharp-eyed gobblers. Then there's the old saw about setting up above, or on the same level with, a gobbler in hill country. It's a good rule of thumb, though I'm sure I'm far from the only turkey hunter to have occasionally called turkeys downhill.

Knowing the area can help hunters avoid the common mistake of setting up with something between themselves and a gobbler that will tend to hang them up—fences, streams, ravines, and so forth. On the flip side, the knowledge of logging roads, ridgetop trails, pastures, and similar features can help hunters visualize exactly where a turkey is gobbling from, where he's headed, and what route he'll use to get there, all of which can obviously be helpful in selecting a setup.

All these points being made, the fact remains that more often than not, when I hear a gobbler sound off, I find myself wondering where to set up. If the bird is close, the search can be somewhat frantic. And wherever I choose to sit, I'm almost sure to see a slightly better spot just 10 or 15 yards away.

This subject of where to set up when turkey hunting isn't one I hear discussed often among turkey hunters, unless I bring it up. I'm still fascinated by it, still looking for the perfect setup. Rarely do I spend time with experienced turkey hunters without eventually getting around to the subject. I want to know if they prefer a wide-open vista, permitting them to observe the gobblers at long range, or a setup from which a gobbler can't see them until he's within shotgun range. I want to know how closely they attempt to approach a gobbler on the roost in various situations. I want to know if they grab a spot at the first gobble, or take time to find the best possible spot. And what about blind calling? Would a spot they selected for blind calling resemble a spot they'd select when a gobbler was sounding off and on the way in?

I asked some of our experts these questions, and here are their responses.

Paul Butski warms immediately to the subject of setting up on turkeys. It's his specialty. Few decisions are more important, Butski says, than where a hunter chooses to set up. Pick the right spot—the spot the bird wants come to—and you shoot the turkey. Pick the wrong spot, you don't.

Wrong spots are easier to identify than right spots. If an obstruction hangs the gobbler up and he doesn't get within shotgun range, it's the wrong spot. If limbs or brush obstruct vision or prevent moving the gun into position, it's the wrong spot.

"Early on as a turkey hunter, I tended to seek too much concealment," admits Butski. "I wanted to be hidden, and too often I couldn't see well or couldn't get the gun into position at the critical moment. One big problem with spots like this is that they cause too much movement. All that peeking around to see under a limb or around a bush, or to get the gun in position with something in the way, causes movement that turkeys will spot."

If Butski agrees with me about the importance of selecting the right setup, he's got my number on another issue.

"A lot of turkey hunters have problems because they're indecisive about selecting setups. They want to find that perfect spot, and they spend too much time doing it, or they move around too much getting to it. Sometimes you have plenty of time to get set up, but often you don't. If that bird is coming in, you don't have any time. The thing to do is drop and get ready. Figure out where the turkey is, how far away he is, how fast he's coming in. Then, if you have time and want to move, move."

What's the right spot? Any spot that isn't a wrong spot, of course.

Butski likes to close the distance on birds. If terrain or foliage permits, he closes to 125, or even 100, yards. If the bird is on the ground and answers a call when Butski is prospecting, and if the turkey seems to be headed his way, he'll set up as quickly as possible. If the bird is at some distance, or doesn't seem to be moving toward him right away, he'll begin moving toward the bird, calling as he goes.

"I think moving toward the gobbler and calling creates the illusion to the gobbler that the hen is doing what hens often do—responding to his gobbling and heading toward him. That's a very natural situation, and very realistic to the gobbler."

It's a risky tactic, he concedes, but he feels that, done carefully, the risk is worthwhile to help complete the illusion and to close the distance on the bird. Butski will keep tabs on the bird as he moves, of course, and when the time is right, he'll drop and set up.

Another important aspect of setting up for Butski is that the right spot can help fill tags when gobblers are unresponsive.

Closing the distance is tough in the wide-open spaces frequently encountered in the West. Hunters must often wait for the birds to come in from great distances.

Like Eddie Salter, Butski believes turkeys can be patterned. Figuring out where gobblers go and when is always helpful, but particularly when a cold front or a gaggle of hens makes gobblers unresponsive to calling. In these situations the hunter who sets up in the right spot and exercises patience still has a good chance to bag a longbeard.

Famous for his aggressive, independent turkey hunting style, Eddie Salter goes by the book when it comes to setting up on gobblers. In hill country he tries as a general rule to set up above gobblers or on their level, but more specifically he has a preference for setting up near the crest of the hill.

"Early in the season, when there's little foliage, I'm careful not to get too close to a gobbler—I think 200 to 250 yards is about right. Later on, with more foliage on the trees, I might cut that distance in half.

"Getting close can be an advantage, but hunters should keep in mind that if you get too close and spook the bird, your hunt for that turkey is about over. Not only that, but you're helping to educate that bird, which will make him warier and more call shy in the future. But if you start out farther away, the bird might still come in from a distance, and if he doesn't you can always relocate."

Eddie avoids setting up in very open areas with almost unlimited visibility. It's not because he fears being seen by the gobbler, though this is always a concern.

"When that ol' gobbler gets to a certain point, he expects to see the hen that's been calling to him. When he doesn't, he's likely to hang up."

When setting up in such an area is unavoidable, Eddie believes a decoy can often be helpful. Better to avoid setting up in such areas when possible, though.

Like Paul Butski, Eddie refers to seeking too much concealment in his setups in his early years of turkey hunting. Eddie was hunting years before the development of modern camo, before wearing head nets and gloves was considered a necessity. Small wonder that hunters in those days tended to sit behind blowdowns, trees, stumps, or other kinds of natural cover.

"I tried to hide too well," Eddie explains, "and it really limited my shot opportunities. Nowadays a hunter in camo can sit in the open, and if he doesn't move a turkey won't usually see him."

For Dick Kirby, setting up is all about making it as easy as possible for the turkey to come to you. That means, among other things, using roads, trails, open patches, and other turkey thruways. It also means keeping potential barriers in mind and setting up, whenever possible, so that a turkey need not cross a stream, ravine, or other obstacle to come in.

Kirby has an interesting observation about setups and turkey behavior.

"In hill country or mountains," he says, "hunters set up in bowls, on steps or ledges, or near ridgetops. Ideally they want to be on a level with the bird or above it, but sometimes they're going to end up calling a bird that's above them, and sometimes those birds will come in.

"The thing to be aware of, for those birds above or below you, is that they never come in on the diagonal. The turkey is always going to go straight across, until he's directly above you or directly below you, then come straight up or straight down. He will not go at an angle."

Finally, Kirby has discovered that sleeping can be an effective way to set up on turkeys.

"Sometimes," he says, "I just *scream* on a call, wait a few minutes, and go to sleep. I can't tell you how many times I've done that and awakened to gobblers close by. It's very effective. Give it a chance. Get in the right area and raise Cain, then go to sleep. It works, I'm tellin' ya."

Larry Norton prefers setups that allow him to see the bird he's calling as much as possible.

"I think it's a big advantage to be able to see that turkey," Larry contends. "I want to know how he's reacting to my calls. That gives me a better idea of how and when to call. I want to know if he's strutting or sneaking in, if he's coming in a hurry or taking his time. I want to know if there are hens or jakes or other gobblers with him. And if he loses interest or runs off with a hen, I know it if I can see him and I adjust my strategy accordingly, and don't waste time sitting in a spot for an hour and calling to a bird that's not there."

Note how the part of the hunter that is shaded is nearly invisible, while the portion in the light is easily seen.

He acknowledges that gobblers will sometimes hang up in an open area when they don't see the hen that has been calling to them, but Larry believes he has a cure for this problem.

"I try to set up with some kind of obstruction out in front of me that the gobbler can't see through. It might be a bush, or a blowdown, or a little hill, or it might even be just a few big trees growing together. That way the gobbler won't wonder why he can't see the hen and hang up. He'll just assume she's behind that obstruction. Sometimes he'll go right to it looking for her."

Why not use decoys? They're illegal in Alabama, where Larry guides and does most of his turkey hunting. He recommends their use wherever they're legal.

"An unspooked turkey is much easier to call than one that knows you're there," cautions Matt Morrett. "How close I get to a turkey really depends on the terrain and how well I know the area I'm hunting. I try to get as close as possible in situations where I know the lay of the land. If I'm unfamiliar with the area, I would rather not push my luck and spook a gobbling turkey.

"I prefer to get to an area where I know the turkey can get to me—openings, logging roads, and ridgetops are great areas to set up in, but don't let that gobbler be able to see your location or there's a good chance he'll want you to come to him and not commit to your location."

A fairly aggressive turkey hunter, Morrett doesn't believe in devoting excessive time to any one gobbler in most situations.

"Relocation to me is a kind of gut feeling. Honestly, if a turkey doesn't respond or commit, providing I know that there are more birds in the area, I may give him 30 minutes, then move on. One thing for sure, though—I will pay him a visit later that morning to see if he's lonely."

When the Woods Are Silent

Every turkey hunter has been there. It's a beautiful spring morning, and the air is filled with the scent of wildflowers and emerging foliage, damp earth and pine needles. The whippoorwills are calming down as the songbirds take over, and it's light enough now to see fog lifting out of the valley. Any moment that first electrifying gobble of the morning is sure to ring out.

But you always expect it too soon, you remind yourself. It usually doesn't come until you've begun to worry that it won't.

There it is! Nope, that's a dog barking somewhere.

Okay, it's time for the locator call.

Nothing.

Time to try it again.

Still nothing. Nothing and nothing.

This is not what we expect when we roll out of bed at some evil hour to go climb hills, wade streams, or slog through swamps with a flashlight. It happens, though. Sometimes bad weather accounts for it, but other times the gobblers just . . . aren't gobbling.

Sometimes, I suspect they're just not there. Over the years of traveling to hunt out of various camps and lodges, often with half a dozen to a dozen turkey hunters going out daily, I've noticed a frequent pattern. On a given day, assuming good weather, a few smiling hunters are probably going to come into camp with gobblers. A few others will return with stories of epic duels and near misses. And a few disgruntled hunters will return to complain that they couldn't buy a gobble, nothing going on, didn't see any turkeys.

Turkeys do move, and one has to suspect that the turkeys simply weren't in the areas where the unlucky hunters hunted.

My friend Tom Cross, a southern Ohio native who helped introduce me to turkey hunting more years ago than I like to remember, has a different theory.

"Sometimes I think the gobblers in a certain area just don't get fired up. If one of them gets cranked up and starts gobbling, the others join in. If the one that usually gets things cranked up is in somebody's freezer, or maybe just roosting somewhere else, the other gobblers in the area just never get fired up enough to start gobbling."

There's no doubt that turkeys are sometimes present but not gobbling—you bump one walking down a logging road, maybe, or you spot them feeding or strutting in a field. For reasons that perhaps only they know, they're just not gobbling.

What happens more often than no gobbling, and can be almost equally discouraging, are those days on which you hear a little gobbling on the roost, but the birds clam up after flydown. That can be an indication that gobblers are henned up; then again, it can happen seemingly anytime during the season.

The question, of course, is what to do about it. A surprising number of hunters get bored and leave the woods after a couple of hours of no gobbling activity. It occurs to me from time to time that perhaps outdoor writers and turkey hunting experts should quit telling hunters not to do that. It's a major mistake, of course, to leave the woods early, but those who do it are leaving the woods, and the gobblers, to those more dedicated, more persistent hunters who arguably are more deserving.

Harvest statistics reveal that far and away the most gobblers are taken in the first 30 minutes to one hour after first light. But my personal harvest statistics reveal that in Ohio and Indiana, for instance, where hunting is limited to the morning hours, I've taken as many gobblers between the hours of nine and noon as I have between first light and nine o'clock. Most of the experienced turkey hunters I speak with report similar experiences. The statewide harvest statistics can be so skewed for only one reason: Most hunters apparently leave the woods early. Few gobblers are taken late in the morning only because few hunters are there pursuing them.

Most hunters apparently assume that because gobbling activity is diminished, the chances of bringing a tom to the gun are equally diminished. Not so.

As any expert will tell you, the gobbler that responds to calling later in the morning is more likely to come to the call than is the early bird. Presumably, this is because hens often leave the gobblers later in the morning, and the gobblers get lonely. Stay in the woods, calling regularly, and sooner or later, even after two or three hours of no gobbling, a tom will sound off and catch you so completely by surprise your hair will stand on end. The heat of the late-morning sun, the bugs, the blisters, the sore muscles, the lack of sleep, the hours of relative boredom—all will be quickly forgotten when you hear that second gobble and realize it's closer than was the first one, and that tom is headed your way.

Then, too, gobblers don't always betray their presence by gobbling. Plenty of them, possibly even most of them, sneak in

The weather was perfect, but no birds were gobbling. What did the author do? He stayed put until late morning, when this tom suddenly appeared from out of nowhere.

silently. These are the truly challenging ones, and though they don't fulfill our fantasy of the longbeard strutting, gobbling, and drumming his way into a load of No. 6 shot, the hunter who has remained patient and alert enough to take one of these birds has more reason for pride in the accomplishment, in my opinion, than if the tom had come in strutting and gobbling all the way and all but offering himself for sacrifice.

Most of the experts with whom I raised this issue responded initially with a long silence. Could be that some of them are so blessed by good areas with very high populations of turkeys that they rarely encounter this problem. More likely, I suspect, it's a difficult problem and addressing it requires some thought.

Several of the conversations started along these lines:

"You say no turkeys are gobbling at all?"

"Right."

"Hmmmmm. None at all, eh? Hmmmm. That's a tough one."

Eddie Salter, not surprisingly, responds to this problem by hunting even more aggressively than usual.

"Sometimes," he says, "they're just not there. When they're not there, move. Cover some ground, and keep moving. I call, and I call aggressively. You have to believe you can find a turkey somewhere, and you will. Occasionally I'll stop and call for 15 minutes, then I'll move on."

Eddie likes to remind the audiences at his turkey hunting seminars that sometimes, when the hunting is tough in the spring, hunters can resort to fall hunting tactics.

"A lot of hunters think that if they bump some turkeys off the roost, or they come around a turn in a logging road and spook a gobbler with some hens, they might as well move on and look for other birds in another area. That can be a big mistake.

"If those birds get scattered, the gobbler wants to get back together with the hens. You might have to wait for an hour, and you might need to relocate a time or two, but if you start yelpin' and that gobbler starts back toward you gobblin', you're in for home cookin'."

If the gobbler doesn't return to the area, but gobbles and continues gobbling, Eddie advises hunters to stay with him and continue relocating and calling as often as necessary to work the bird in.

John McDaniel is direct and to the point.

"In that situation, I call blind," he says matter-of-factly. "I set up in a good spot and call for 20 minutes or so."

John often hunts big-woods birds, where populations may be less concentrated than is the case in some regions. He believes in covering ground.

"If I'm really confident in that spot—maybe it's a big basin, where the sound of my call carries well and I think I can call a turkey from a long distance—I'll give the spot 45 minutes. That amount of time is very ample if you're not hearing any gobbling."

Tim Hooey is a big guy who stays in excellent shape, has seemingly endless energy, and clearly has a real passion for turkey hunting. All this seems somehow inconsistent with his laid-back style of turkey hunting, but this unaggressive approach to turkey hunting is reflected in the way he approaches hunting when the gobblers are silent.

"The first thing I do when gobblers aren't sounding off spontaneously, or responding to calls, is switch calls," says Hooey. "If the call I'm using isn't working, it's time to go to another one. Maybe the gobblers know that call, but whatever the reason, it isn't working. Sometimes you go through a whole range of calls, getting no response, and then suddenly *wham!* There he is."

Hooey's calling style, like his overall approach to turkey hunting, is not aggressive. When he's talking about switching calls, he's talking about changing from a mouth call to a box call, a box call to a slate call, and so on. He rarely cutts or uses similar emotional, high-energy types of calls.

"The next thing I'll do is sit. I don't prospect much. I'll just go to the spot where the turkeys will show up, and I'll sit there, and now and then I'll cluck, purr, or make soft yelps. I scratch the leaves once in a while, too. Many hunters may not think of that as a call, but I do. Scratching is a great call."

I mentioned in chapter 2, on scouting, that Peter Fiduccia practices minimum-impact scouting for turkeys. I should point out that this is my impression of Peter's style, and not a description he uses himself. In any case, he hunts in much the same way, with an eye always toward not alerting birds, spooking them, educating them, or altering their normal behavior patterns in any way.

"I abandon all sexual vocalizations," Peter says in explaining his approach to hunting turkeys when gobblers are unresponsive. "Instead, I use soft feeding purrs from a hen. I want to convey soft, content feeding and browsing sounds.

"Usually, if I don't bring in a gobbler, I'll bring in one or more hens. When that happens it doesn't take long for a gobbler to show up."

Peter does caution hunters about one particular challenge associated with this style of hunting. Since gobblers may be slipping in silently at any time, it's essential to remain as close to absolutely motionless as possible. This is especially true when hens respond to the calling, and any number of sharp eyes may be in the immediate vicinity as a gobbler makes his way in.

*   *   *

"Two miles down the road can make a world of difference," advises Matt Morrett, suggesting that covering ground to find a fired-up gobbler is his preferred strategy when the woods are too quiet. Of course, in many areas hunters are limited to small private properties.

"If moving is not an option," Matt says, "I'll try to think what the turkeys are most likely doing at that time—feeding, going to water, strutting, et cetera. I'll spend a lot of time listening and not calling to devise my plan. Sometimes a coin toss may work, also."

12

Hunting the Slam

I cannot explain the fascination with the various hunting slams, but I have succumbed to it nearly to the point of obsession on more than one occasion. Years ago, on a northern Ontario waterfowl hunt with *Outdoor Secrets* host Babe Winkelman, I bagged a blue-winged teal and a green-winged teal on the same morning.

"You know," Babe observed as we compared the two drakes, "if you had a cinnamon teal you could have the three birds mounted together on a pedestal of some kind. That would be all three of the North American teal. It would make a neat display."

Cinnamon teal are West Coast birds, rarely ranging as far east as the prairie states. I actually made tentative plans to book a hunt out West, just to get that diminutive bird and claim . . . what? A Teal Slam?

My friend and blackpowder writer Hank Strong, who loves to hunt wild hogs with his smokepole, often speaks of promoting a Ham Slam, but he hasn't yet figured out what it will consist of.

Doubtless many thousands of turkey hunters find sufficient excitement and challenge in hunting the local subspecies of turkey, and feel no particular need to hunt the others. More than a few expert turkey hunters have no burning desire to travel to various parts of the continent just to be able to claim the Grand Slam (all four American subspecies), the Royal Slam (those four plus the Mexican Gould's turkey), or the World Slam (the previous five plus a separate species of turkey found in Central America, the Ocellated turkey).

Many other turkey hunters accept the challenge. For some, it may be a competitive streak that prompts the quest—nor is there anything wrong with that, so long as it doesn't become obsessive or lead to unethical hunting practices or a lack of respect for the game. We all like to catch the biggest fish, or the most fish, or take a bigger buck, or shoot our limit of doves first,

The Sierra Madres of Mexico are home to the Gould's turkey. Big, rugged country makes mules a welcome asset on some Gould's turkey hunts.

Author with a Gould's turkey.

but I suspect that for most hunters, hunting the slam is more a matter of setting goals and enjoying a sense of accomplishment.

For me, love of travel is a big factor. Not only do I enjoy hunting turkeys in environments ranging from swamps to mountains, deserts, and prairies, but I also like being in those different places and even just getting to them.

Many turkey hunters like to discuss the various subspecies and talk about the differences among them—not the obvious differences in appearance, but any perceived differences in the way they behave, the sounds they make, the calls they respond best to, the hunting strategies that are required to take them consistently. Other hunters, including some of our experts, are inclined to downplay the differences.

As of this writing, Dick Kirby has completed 38 turkey Grand Slams, 19 of them consecutive. The man obviously knows all the subspecies. Kirby is among those who tends to downplay any real differences among them, believing that the perceived differences have more to do with the hunting pressure to which they are subjected and the different environments they inhabit than with any inherent characteristics.

"They do gobble a little differently," he concedes. "A Rio, for instance, has more of a yodeling quality to its gobble. Calling to them is the same, though.

"I also think it may be true that Osceolas tend to be a little more leery than other subspecies, and that through most of the spring season, they tend to gobble less.

"The biggest factor is hunting pressure. I don't care where you hunt or what kind of turkey you're after, the one that has been hunted hardest is the one that's going to be the toughest to get. You might go to a big private ranch in Florida where the hunting is very limited, and if you get there when the gobbling activity is

Author with Osceola.

at a peak, you may get your Osceola very quickly. At the same time, you might go to Texas, where the Rio Grande gobblers are often thought to be the least challenging of the subspecies, and if you're hunting an area that has been hunted heavily, you can have a very tough time bagging that Rio gobbler."

There are several things Kirby recommends by way of preparation for hunting the different subspecies.

"Many hunters who haven't traveled widely aren't prepared for the sometimes very big differences in weather or terrain. The heat can be intense in the more southerly locations, and heavy clothes that are perfect for the Northeast or the Midwest make for terribly uncomfortable conditions in the South. Depending on where you're going, you might need to be prepared for bugs. Hunters traveling out West might find conditions more physically demanding. And they might need different boots than the swamp waders they're accustomed to."

Different types of terrain can demand different hunting strategies.

"A few years ago I took some friends from Pennsylvania on a Texas Rio hunt in flat, wide-open country. Turkeys were everywhere. I dropped them off at a spot where they had 3,000 acres to hunt. When I picked them up on day one, neither had a turkey. I said to 'em, 'You guys are walking, aren't you? You can't do that out here. The birds can see you from 500 yards away. They'll come to you, but you can't really go after them in this area.'

"Next day, same thing: Neither of them has a turkey though other hunters in camp are bagging birds. I went out with them the third day, and they both got their turkeys. It was just hard for them to learn that in that wide-open country, they couldn't move in on turkeys the way they do in the Pennsylvania hardwoods."

Kirby is convinced that a lot of traveling hunters are disappointed because they aren't selective enough in picking an outfitter.

"Look, you don't have to bag a turkey to have a successful hunt. But at the same time, you don't want to spend the money and the time and hunt where your chances are low because the outfitter hasn't done his job.

"These days there are a lot of outfitters conducting what I call 'Wal-Mart' hunts. They book too many hunters and over-hunt the area they have. The first guys there have decent hunts, and after that they go downhill. I don't care how good the place is, if it's been hunted every day for 20 days prior to your arrival, your chances aren't good. You're probably going to hear very little if any gobbling, and you're not likely to see turkeys, let alone get a shot at them.

"The cost of a hunt isn't a reliable indicator of the quality, either. You can pay a lot for a lousy hunt, and some quality hunts are very affordable. You have to do your homework. Ask a lot of questions. Ask how many hunters they book, and how much land they have to hunt on. An outfitter should have refer-

While successful hunts don't have to end with
dead birds, it's nice when they do.

ences, and hunters should check a number of them. I don't care how famous the place is, or how big the ads are. Check the references.

"I recommend hunters book a minimum of four or five days at each place they hunt. Give yourself a fair chance, and keep in mind that you can easily lose a few days to weather. Along the same lines, I'm surprised at how many hunters quit early, and don't hunt all day. If you have the option, hunt all day. You can kill a turkey any time of the day, but not if you're back at the lodge taking a nap."

Tim Hooey is convinced that the calls of the various subspecies have their own distinctive sounds.

"Hunters can listen to yelps on turkey hunting videos and hear the differences," insists Hooey, who recently took a bow Grand Slam in one season. "For instance, I've yet to hear a Rio or a Merriam's with a raspy call. They're higher pitched, and maybe with a little quicker cadence.

"Rio gobblers seem to like higher-pitched calling, especially. I like to use friction calls when Rio hunting for that reason. Those little pushpin calls work really well on Rios. A lot of guys don't like them, think they're kids' calls or something. I say, 'Fine, don't use 'em. I'll use 'em and they'll work better for me because I'm the only one.' "

Hooey especially enjoys hunting the Merriam's turkey, often regarded as being the most vocal of the subspecies. Normally a laid-back, unaggressive caller, Hooey makes an exception for Merriam's, which he thinks respond better to aggressive calling.

Apart from that, any adjustments in Hooey's hunting styles for the various subspecies seem to have more to do with the local environment than with differences among the subspecies.

"Turkeys in hot areas, like Texas Rios, really look for shade at midday. I've been in situations where we could just glass for

Many hunters believe that the Merriam's is the most beautiful of the turkey subspecies.

them in shady spots, then move in close to call them out of the shade. Sometimes they come on the run when you do that.

"Osceolas seek shade, too. They like the hammocks, or cypress heads, adjacent to fields. Generally, though, I'll hunt Osceolas the same way I hunt Eastern gobblers."

Hooey offers a final pointer on the subject of hunting the various subspecies.

"All turkeys will orient to water," he asserts. "They like to roost over it, and they move up and down creek bottoms, just like deer. When in doubt, look for water."

Preparing for the slam, in Steve Puppe's opinion, is largely a matter of paying attention to the differences in climates and using appropriate clothing and gear for the climate. Clearly, a hunter planning a hunt for Osceolas in Florida or Rio Grandes in South Texas will want to be prepared for warm, or even hot, weather,

Swamp buggies are often used in pursuit of Florida turkeys.

while a hunter planning a hunt for Merriam's in Wyoming or Easterns in Vermont should be prepared for a cooler climate.

As a personal aside, experience compels me to caution hunters not to assume the South is always warm and the North is always cold. Spring weather is fickle just about everywhere, and more than a few Yankees have sat shivering in the South in unseasonably cool weather, while temperatures even on the plains of South Dakota can soar to unexpected highs on a sunny day.

"Hunters should also be aware of the possibility of elevation when hunting Merriam's in a mountain state," advises Puppe. What kind of preparation does this entail? It probably means wearing lighter boots with good ankle support, for one thing, as opposed to the knee-highs better suited for wading streams or slogging down muddy logging roads.

It might mean lighter gear in general, to the extent possible—using a fanny pack instead of a day pack, for instance, or even carrying a light autoloader instead of a heavy double-bore.

Rio Grandes are sometimes thought to be the least challenging of the turkey subspecies, but many experts attribute this to lower hunting pressure.

And then there's the simple matter of physical conditioning. Even hunters accustomed to climbing big hills in the Appalachians will probably find that the thinner air at higher western elevations is more demanding than anything they're accustomed to. And for flatlanders, the combination of steep terrain and thin air can be truly challenging.

Does Puppe perceive any differences among the various subspecies? He's in the clear majority on that question.

"I feel that the Eastern and Osceola turkeys are probably the most difficult to take because of their shy nature. Merriam's and Rios are generally more eager to respond to a call."

Puppe is quick to identify his favorite turkey hunting spot.

"I would have to say my favorite place to hunt would be in the Black Hills of South Dakota, for Merriam's."

Matt Morrett is inclined to agree with Puppe and many hunters about the beauty of Merriam's turkeys, though he has a different, if less specific spot in mind for hunting them.

"There is nothing more beautiful than a Merriam's longbeard in full strut in the mountains of the western United States," muses Morrett.

"Personally, though, I love to hunt Eastern turkeys best. I believe they're the most challenging subspecies as far as turkeys go."

Afternoon Delight

There's something very civilized about turkey hunting hours that end at noon or one o'clock. It's a little like dry-fly fishing for trout—no point being out there till the sun hits the water and the hatch starts, so why not sleep in and enjoy a leisurely breakfast?

Not that turkey hunting allows for sleeping in, of course. There's no getting around the need to roll out of bed while the stars are still shining. On the flip side, though, it's nice to stop for lunch at the end of the hunt. Time to recount the morning's adventures over a sandwich and a cold beverage, maybe nap after lunch, do a little fishing in the pond, throw a steak on the grill. No guilt about not being in the woods; hunting is not an option. No concerns that *your* gobbler is even now thrilling some other nimrod, double-gobbling and strutting his way to a date with the payload of a Remington Magnum. Wake up refreshed the next morning and eager to hunt.

Contrast this with day four of a turkey hunt in a state that permits all-day turkey hunting. Long before first light you stumble to the bathroom and peek into the mirror through bloodshot, sleep-starved eyes at a stubble-covered face that looks years older than it did a few long days ago. There's a blister on your heel and a splinter in your hand. Your back hurts, your butt is sore, and your legs ache. You find yourself standing in the hall staring at the floor, and wonder if you've been doing that for two minutes or twenty. You stagger to the kitchen table, already occupied by a hunched over gaggle of similar-looking desperadoes. One is staring into his coffee, another at the floor, the third at you. The one staring at you was best man in your wedding twenty years ago, but you can't remember his name, and he doesn't appear to recognize you. Oh, the humanity!

Arguably, I guess, dealing with sleep deprivation is part of the challenge of turkey hunting. Maybe a turkey hunter is *supposed* to feel physically and emotionally drained at the end of the hunt, more relieved than elated as he slings a big gobbler over his shoulder for the hike down the mountain. Nah.

Okay, maybe it's an age thing. I can't be sure, because when I was a younger man I hunted in a tristate area and all three states limited turkey hunting to half a day. I never had the opportunity to hunt turkeys all day as a young man.

These days, when I'm hunting in one of those all-day states, I work extra hard at bagging a tom that first or second day of the hunt. Then I can return to camp and nap, maybe even sleep in the next morning to get caught up, before heading out again.

It's only fair to say this, though: In morning-only states, I've bagged quite a few gobblers very late in the morning, and in all-day states, I've bagged a few toms late in the afternoon. The birds are out there, and they can be brought to the gun at any time of the day. The hunter who has the option of hunting all day and doesn't take advantage of it is significantly reducing his chances for success.

*According to Butski, open areas seem particularly popular
in the afternoon. This gobbler is in full strut.*

Many hunters believe that, though gobblers sound off less in the afternoon, the hunter who does get one to gobble in response to a call has a better chance of bringing this bird in than is the case in the morning. Paul Butski agrees with these hunters.

"Often," Butski opines, "turkeys are in the fields in the afternoon, which makes them easy to locate."

Another thing Butski likes about hunting gobblers in the afternoon is that, even when they're with hens, the hens seem to pay less attention to them in the afternoon. That's a great point to remember on those frustrating days when the gobblers all seem to be henned up. Locating gobblers can be tough when they're not gobbling, which is often the case when they have hens. Even when they can be located, calling them away from hens isn't easy. By glassing fields in the afternoon, hunters have an opportunity to locate these quiet gobblers, and at a time when they may be more inclined to leave the hens.

Butski adjusts his afternoon hunting style to something he describes as less aggressive, more laid back.

"I don't call less aggressively," he says to clarify the point, "but I move less aggressively, and I set up longer. I do that because I think gobblers are more likely to come in silently in the afternoon than in the morning."

Larry Norton does most of his hunting in Alabama, far from Butski's haunts in the Northeast. But his strategy for hunting afternoon gobblers is similar.

"For evening hunting," says Larry, "I like to concentrate around fields. Turkeys spend a lot of time feeding in fields in the afternoon. They want to fill up before it's time to roost.

"Often I'll just go from one green field to another looking for gobblers. I love to find them already in the field. If he has

Locating turkeys headed to roost can help dramatically when you go out the next morning.

done his homework, scouted before the season, and paid attention to what's going on during the season, a hunter can usually
have a pretty good idea where that gobbler is headed to roost
after feeding time. I'll try to set up in that direction. I don't call
aggressively, I just make a lot of contented feeding sounds.

"A lot of times when they're feeding like that, they're not
going to move. They're not going to come out of that field until
they've fed; then they take off and they don't stop. If I've set up
in the right place, they'll walk right to me.

"After about four o'clock, if I haven't located any birds, I'll
pick a spot to set up and call quietly until dark. If I don't bring a
bird in, I might at least roost some, and then I know where I'll
be hunting next morning."

"Honestly," concedes Matt Morrett, "when I chase afternoon turkeys, I'm doing it in areas where I believe the turkeys
are going to show up on their way to roost. I still try to locate
them on my way in, but I usually just find myself an area to
spend the evening in.

"Afternoon hunting can be productive, but the best part is
that it can really help you the next morning. Roosting turkeys
can help dramatically, especially in areas where you're unfamiliar with the terrain. Hearing a turkey gobble the night before
your hunt can also help a lot with the motivation factor, especially if you're worn out."

Fall Turkey Hunting

Let me say up front that fall turkey hunting is not my bag. This could change. I haven't done a great deal of fall turkey hunting, in part because in the fall of the year I hunt deer, upland game, and waterfowl, and much as I enjoy the attempt, I find a man just can't do it all.

When I have hunted fall turkeys, it has usually been with my smokepole. I'm not sure why—something about Thanksgiving, I suppose, and the sense of tradition it inspires. Never really a buckskinner type, I find that something about hunting turkeys in the fall makes me inclined to reach for the old caplock fouling piece and think of wearing moccasins instead of boots, a fur hat instead of my camo baseball-style cap.

For years I've insisted that the spring gobblers that get fired up and come in gobbling and strutting all the way are the easy ones, while the sly old gobbler that sneaks in silently is the real challenge. I believe this, but nonetheless I head for the woods in the spring with the same visions of strutting, drumming, double-gobbling longbeards as most other spring turkey hunters.

Less challenging or not, it's still a thrill to me to hear a gobbler making his way through the woods to where I'm sitting against an oak tree, gun already shouldered. As my friend Russ Markesbery once described it, "It's like a monster is coming through the woods to get you."

And the sight of a gobbler in full strut, red, white, and blue head almost unnaturally vivid against the pastel colors of spring, is still a sight I can't take my eyes from. The sound of a gobbler spitting and drumming almost mesmerizes me. No wonder many Native Americans believed turkeys were mystical birds with supernatural powers.

Obviously, all this is not a part of fall turkey hunting.

But for a growing number of hunters, fall turkey hunting is as exciting in its way as is spring turkey hunting. The fall woods feature their own beauty. Many find that fall hunting is a little more laid back; young-of-the-year turkeys frantically seeking a reunion

Finding and scattering family flocks is the most
common approach to fall turkey hunting.

are a little less demanding of hunters than are spring gobblers. And while fall gobblers are widely considered to be more challenging than their counterparts in the spring, calling them usually requires more patience and a less aggressive approach.

Here's what some of our experts had to say about fall turkey hunting.

Matt Morrett is convinced that simply locating turkeys is the key to fall hunting success. Morrett tries to find their food sources, and perhaps water sources in an arid location or a dry year. Upon locating birds, he follows the common practice of scattering the flock and trying to regroup them using young lost-turkey sounds such as kee-kees and yelps.

"I never want to sound like Mama, though," Morrett cautions. "Those young birds know their mother's voice."

Morrett agrees that hunting fall gobblers is a supreme challenge.

"For old gobblers, you put your deer hunting shoes on. You scout smart, keep calling to a minimum, using gobbler clucks and yelps, and pray for a little luck."

Despite the very high degree of importance Morrett attaches to calling when it comes to hunting spring gobblers, Morrett feels differently about their counterparts in the fall.

"Hunting mature gobblers in the fall is definitely about hunting, not calling," he admits.

"No matter where you hunt turkeys, they tend to live in the same areas year after year," opines Dick Kirby. "In most places, if turkeys are present in an area in the spring, they'll be in that area, or not far away, in the fall. They do tend to habituate to crops, though, like corn and soybeans, and these change from one year to the next, so hunters need to be aware of those changes.

"There is no denying that fall hunting for mature gobblers is more challenging than hunting them in the spring. I usually start hunting fall turkeys by looking for fresh scratchings. That will tell you the turkeys are in that location.

"Sometimes a gobbler call will get them to respond. The gobbler's yelp is a slow, deep, raspier kind of yelp than a hen yelp. When I hear gobblers vocalizing in the woods, I try to duplicate what they do. If they're clucking, I cluck. If they're yelping, I yelp. And put some personality into it.

"Often you end up just blind calling. I like to use a boat paddle. I might yelp a few times, then sit 20 minutes. Gradually, I'll call a little louder. Basically for fall gobbler hunting, you have to call less and be more patient."

Kirby relates the following incident about a fall gobbler hunt many years ago.

"I was using one of those old, round Penn's Woods slate calls, and I was very new to turkey hunting. I looked way down the hill, and here comes a big gobbler. My gun was leaning against the tree, and every time the gobbler passed behind something, I'd move that gun a little, to get it in position. Eventually I got it in position, but the gobbler stopped about 50 yards out, and wouldn't budge. I thought he was never going to move, and eventually I almost gave up on him. I had put the call in my pocket when the gobbler closed in, and suddenly it fell out of my pocket and rolled down the hill a ways. I thought it would spook the gobbler, but instead he must have thought it was a turkey scratching in the leaves. He ran right at me and I shot him."

Roger Raisch is a great enthusiast of fall turkey hunting. As he does with spring hunting, Roger emphasizes the importance of scouting for fall turkeys. Like Lovett Williams, Roger scouts not only during the off season, but also during the season as he hunts. In the early fall he often concentrates on the same places he hunts turkeys in the spring.

"Open woods, logging roads, and pastures, where grasshoppers and other insects are found, are excellent places to locate turkey sign in early fall," observes Raisch.

"During late fall in colder climates, birds spend more time in the woods scratching in the leaves for acorns, seeds, and other food. They also spend a lot more time then in harvested grain fields.

"Fall flocks are usually easy to locate by all the calling and noise they make moving around, and when they fly up in the evening and fly down in the morning. I find that they usually engage in a turkey fight or two in the morning, and often an hour or so before roost time. The sounds of wing flapping, flying from tree to tree, clucking and putting is very easy to hear from a far distance on a quiet evening when they go to roost."

Raisch most enjoys the now traditional strategy of breaking up flocks and calling them back.

"I usually roost a flock, then wait about 20 minutes after they have flown up and are settled down. Then I walk quickly, and as quietly as possible, right into the middle of them. They'll start to fly. When they do, I start clapping my hands together, yelling, and banging a heavy stick on trees to scare all of them into flying at once. They'll fly up to a quarter mile away, going in various directions. Some will only fly 100 or so.

"I return to the roost site about an hour before sunrise the next morning and start my calling. They'll tend to regroup within 50 yards of the roost site. As they regroup, one or more will usually pass by and come to my calling."

For this type of hunting, Roger prefers a three- or four-reed hand-stretched mouth call with a notch or two in one of the reeds, feeling that with this call he can imitate any sound a fall turkey makes, including the high-pitched kee-kee of the young-of-the-year turkeys. The same call will also make the deeper yelps and clucks of mature gobblers.

"I call a lot, imitating just about every sound I hear turkeys make. I don't think you can overcall in the fall, except when dealing with old gobblers.

"Old gobblers," Raisch agrees, "are tough. Tough to locate generally. They stay very quiet and to themselves, away from the noisy hens and young of the year."

They do use the same feeding areas as the other turkeys, Roger points out, so he looks for them in the same places.

"Frankly, I don't target them because I like to hunt them in the spring better, when they are much more exciting to hunt."

When he does locate fall gobblers, Raisch is of the same opinion as other experts: The key to taking them is patience and less frequent, less excited calling. After busting up a flock of fall gobblers, Raisch will often stay in that spot for five hours or more, waiting for the gobblers to regroup. This can sometimes take days, so there is no guarantee of success.

"If that doesn't work," suggests Raisch, "return to the same area a couple of hours before roost time that same day. They may have returned by then and can be called in."

Last-Ditch Tactics

This topic interests me, inherently dramatic as it is. Surely this must be what turkey hunters most want to hear from the experts: What do you do when the conventional methods fail? What tricks do you pull from the bottom of the bag when time is running out? What unheard-of tactics do you resort to when the clock is ticking and the toms just won't respond? What is your secret weapon? Your all-out, last-ditch, no-holds-barred, nothing-to-lose desperation tactic?

Could be this is a classic case of projection. Beginning turkey hunters, I'm sure, are more interested in the basics, but I have to think that any hunters with a few turkey notches on their shotguns are interested in learning what the experts do to fill a tag when nothing else is working.

Their answers may surprise you a little, as they did me, but in retrospect they shouldn't have. I thought about a few of the more memorable, last-minute turkeys I've taken over the years.

There was an Eastern bird I shot ten minutes before the official end of what had been a very long and frustrating Ohio season for me a few years ago. Sure I couldn't pull him across a pasture and into the woods where I sat, and that he couldn't see through a thicket sprouting out of a drainage between us, I raced across the pasture and set up in the thicket to work the bird. I heard a single cluck and knew he was in the pasture behind me, and with minutes left in the season and nothing to lose I rotated on my seat 180 degrees and bowled him over as he ran off.

There was a big Indiana tom I took once at the very end of a hunt. I had stood up and was on the verge of leaving the woods in defeat when a pair of geese flew low over a wheat field in the valley, and their constant ha-ronking prompted a gobble out of a bird I'd been playing cat and mouse with all morning. I slipped a little closer to the gobbler and called quietly for ten minutes when I spotted what looked like a dogwood blossom bobbing through the trees on the hillside below me. It was the white head of the gobbler, of course, and I shot him at 40 yards.

Then there was a Gould's I killed in Mexico on a hunt with Dan Nasca of Caza Loco Outfitters. For half an hour or more that gobbler strutted and gobbled close by, several times coming within 15 yards of me, in a maze of prickly pears that wouldn't allow for a clear shot. Eventually he dropped over a ridge and circled behind me. I crawled to the lip of a saddle in the ridge, peeked down to spot his brilliant red head sticking out from behind a prickly pear, and shot him with a load of #6s.

Thing is, though all those situations themselves seemed dramatic to me, there was nothing dramatically new about the strategies I used. No tricks, no secret methods or startling new tactics. Just an inclination to try something different, or take a risk that I might not take in other situations.

What our experts have to say about last-ditch tactics is simply how they change their strategies when their conventional methods aren't working. There are no startling secrets here, but there are some musings, some adjustments, and yes, a few tricks that might prove useful to you the next time you find yourself in that time-running-out, nothing-to-lose mode of turkey hunting.

"If things are tough, and I need to fill a tag, I go to the grocery store," says Steve Puppe. (Did I mention his droll sense of humor?)

Actually, Puppe's strategy in this situation is similar to Lovett Williams's approach to henned-up gobblers. He stalks them.

"If everything seems to be failing, and birds will not respond to the call for whatever reason, I will have to become a predator and stalk birds very carefully. I'll watch them from a distance to see what they're doing and where they're going, and either sneak on them or get ahead of them and cut them off at the pass."

Puppe is not the only one of our experts who makes reference to stalking turkeys in certain situations, and this probably

*When all else failed, stalking the birds resulted in
two nice gobblers for these hunters.*

merits some comment. The whole issue of stalking turkeys is controversial for three reasons. First, some turkey hunters insist that it's not possible. Second, there are turkey hunters who sincerely believe it's unethical. And finally, there are safety considerations.

The first concern has too often been disproved. Turkeys—especially those that have been subjected to hunting pressure—are extremely wary. Their keen vision is legendary; they're especially quick to spot movement and react to it. They hear very well, too. They aren't supernatural, though. They have no real sense of smell, so being winded is not an issue. Their good hearing is less of a factor than hunters might think. Turkeys in a group tend to be noisy themselves, walking, pecking, scratching in the leaves, and often maintaining a constant stream of low-level clucks, purrs, and yelps. A little wind, or a light rain, can help take hearing out of the picture, too. And it's not unusual for a turkey to hear a hunter and accept the sounds as emanating from another turkey, especially if the hunter is adept at moving quietly and able to enhance the illusion that he's a turkey by pausing frequently, scratching in the leaves occasionally, and purring, clucking, or yelping quietly from time to time.

Their vision may be keen, but they cannot see through rock, despite rumors to the contrary. They cannot see through hills, either, and more than a few turkey hunters have been able to approach turkeys very closely simply by using the terrain to their advantage. In a similar vein, foliage, trees, and other kinds of natural cover can prevent turkeys from taking advantage of their vision. And every experienced turkey hunter knows that turkeys often seek wide-open spaces on windy days because in the woods, the constant movement of trees, limbs, weeds, and foliage makes it difficult for them to spot the movement of predators. The fact is that no game is unstalkable, and turkeys are no exception.

The ethical issue is a trickier subject. Certainly concerns about ethics are to be respected, arguably even applauded. My own feeling—and certainly I'm far from alone in this—is that stalking turkeys, or even waiting them out and bushwhacking them, is a more challenging style of hunting than is calling them in, with the possible exception of mature gobblers in the fall. To hunters who firmly believe that the only way to ethically take a turkey is to sit and call him to the gun, I can only say that I respect their adherence to their code of ethics, but I disagree with them.

The safety issue is a more serious one. Turkey hunting is historically responsible for a disproportionate number of hunting accidents. It's still safer than baseball, bowling, and even pocket billiards according to insurance industry statistics, but one accident is too many. The National Wild Turkey Federation and various other organizations and agencies have done an excellent job of educating turkey hunters about safety issues and reducing the number of turkey hunting accidents, but safety is always a concern.

A friend of mine who was seriously injured in a turkey hunting accident advocates never stalking turkeys, never using gobbler calls, and never using shot sizes bigger than #6 shot. My friend is convinced that he would not be alive today if the "hunter" who shot him in the face had been using #4s. I won't argue with him, but others might point out that if a hunter follows the basic rules of hunting safety, it doesn't matter what size shot he's using.

I once used a low rolling hill in the middle of a large pasture to successfully stalk turkeys, crawling through the clover on one side of the hill to approach within shooting range of a fairly large, noisy flock. I was hunting on carefully controlled private land where I didn't expect to encounter other hunters, but— more to the point—the turkeys weren't within shotgun range of any form of concealment. I was convinced that if another hunter tried to approach them from the side of the hill they were on, he would be exposed and unable to get within range of the birds, and if another hunter had been on my side of the hill, he could not have avoided seeing me.

Ultimately, I'm inclined to leave this issue to the judgment of individual hunters, taking into account the likelihood of encountering other hunters, the presence of which can never be wholly discounted, and the circumstances of a given situation.

Lovett Williams offers a specific and interesting suggestion for a last-ditch strategy that I'm sure I may get around to trying in the future. Lovett is among a dedicated minority of turkey hunters who prefer fall turkey hunting to spring turkey hunting, for the simple reason that he, like many others, believes that ambushing turkeys is a more challenging form of hunting than is calling them in.

"Occasionally," he says, chuckling, "I tear through the woods late in the day after fly-up, while there's still enough light to see. I don't care how much noise I make; the more, the better. I just hurry through areas where I think turkeys might be roosting, trying to flush them and scatter them. When I do, I return and hunt there the next day."

The notion of locating flocks of fall turkeys and flushing them from the roost to scatter them for the next morning's hunt is hardly unusual. It's a favorite tactic of many fall turkey hunters. It's normally done, though, by stealthy hunters who take up listening posts to hear birds flying up on the roost, or by spotting them from a distance across meadows or crop fields. The idea of simply running through the woods until the birds are encountered is one that probably hasn't occurred to most turkey hunters.

"Turkey hunting," says John McDaniel in his book *The American Wild Turkey,* "is a marathon. Be it fall or spring, if you do it the way it should be done, it will test your stamina."

The most successful marathoners usually have a plan. It would seem that running a marathon could not entail a particularly complex plan, but having a plan, and sticking to it, is important. I suspect McDaniel has a plan when he turkey hunts, and that he tends to be disciplined about staying the course. Nonetheless, he does have at least one strategy that he sometimes falls back on when all else fails.

"For years," laments John, "I used to gobble at turkeys as a last resort. Now I'm afraid to."

McDaniel often hunts large tracts of public property near his home in Virginia. While encountering other turkey hunters in the area was once a rarity, it's now common, and McDaniel is justifiably concerned that imitating a gobbler in the spring turkey woods may not be a wise course of action.

"If it's late in the season, and gobblers aren't responding, you can sometimes bring them in if you can yelp like a gobbler—and if you're patient."

McDaniel emphasizes patience, and one other factor that he believes is essential for this strategy to work.

"The gobbler yelp has got to be realistic," he insists. "You can't botch it, or it won't work."

Explaining the difference between a gobbler yelp and a hen yelp is difficult.

"It's partly a matter of timing," McDaniel says. "The gobbler yelp is a little more drawn out, requiring a longer stroke on a box call, for instance. It's more coarse and drawn out, and breaks later than a hen yelp. It has a slower cadence. It's very distinctive."

Usually, according to McDaniel, gobblers tend to sneak in silently to this call. He has also observed that, for whatever reason, it seems very attractive to jakes.

*Ultimately, patience is the key to taking
turkeys, no matter where you hunt.*

"A lot of the birds that come in to this call will be jakes. But
if you're patient, it will bring in gobblers, too. You have to be
very attentive, because they'll come in silently.

"I don't know," he concedes, "if it's curiosity, a desire to join
a bachelor group, or if mating is the motivation, but gobbler
yelping has worked for me in the past in this situation."

Paul Butski responds to last-ditch situations by cranking his
already aggressive hunting style up a notch.

"When you've got nothing to lose, you've got nothing to
lose," he insists. "Get more aggressive with your calling. Try to
close the distance if possible. Take a risk. One way or another in
that situation, I'm going to get a shot—either that, or spook
the bird."

Butski believes some hunters are too afraid to move—not in
the sense of relocating on birds, but in the sense of moving if
necessary to get off a shot. He's convinced some hunters miss

good opportunities for a shot because of an exaggerated sense of how turkeys will react to movement.

"Often you can get away with a little movement," he says, "especially if the turkey goes behind a tree or something. And if a bird is in range and has you pinned down, sometimes you just can't be afraid to move.

"A lot of hunters think they can't possibly shoot a bird that they've spooked with movement, but it can be done. When the time is right, do it in one smooth motion. Just swing and pull the trigger."

Larry Norton's last-ditch tactic entails separating a gobbler from his hens.

"Often hens will roost about 75 yards from the gobbler," he explains. "I'll slip in and flush the hens. Sometimes the gobbler will stay right there. Then I come back to where the hens were and call to the gobbler next morning.

"You've got to pay attention to the gobbler. If he flies off, you need to know which way he went. In that case, I'll go a short distance in that direction next morning to call to him— maybe 70 or 80 yards.

"Whether he stays or leaves, the next morning he's going to be gobbling like crazy. You've got to be in position to get to him before any of those hens do. Sometimes, if you do it right, he'll pitch right down off the roost and into your lap."

Turkey Dogs

Meet the Pros

Gerry Bethge

"Hunting fall turkeys with dogs," says Gerry Bethge, "is my passion." Born in New York, Bethge grew up spending summers at a family cottage in New England, where he learned to fish and hunt. Almost exclusively a white-tailed deer hunter as a young man, Bethge was introduced to spring turkey hunting in 1984 by outdoor writer Mike Pearce and well-known turkey hunter Ray Eye, "almost on a dare." He was hooked on the sport the moment he heard that first gobble, and not long after killed his first turkey a mile from where he'd learned to hunt as a youngster—a place where wild turkeys did not exist during his youth.

Gerry Bethge

Just as Bethge once couldn't imagine a sport more exciting than bowhunting for white-tailed deer, he later couldn't imagine anything more rewarding than hunting spring gobblers. Then, more than a decade ago, he was introduced to fall turkey hunting with dogs.

Currently editor in chief at Harris Publications in New York, Bethge spent 14 years at *Outdoor Life* magazine, the last three as executive editor. He has hunted turkeys across the United States and in Canada.

Pete Clare

Pete Clare hails from Cortland, New York, and was fortunate enough to be born into a hunting family. Pheasants and white-tailed deer were the prominent game species when Pete was a youngster. He graduated from Crawford State in Maryland with a degree in education and returned to New York to spend 10 years teaching and coaching football in the Candor area. He began turkey hunting in the early 1970s, and his passion for hunting and shooting sports led him to leave teaching and open a gun shop. Soon after, in conjunction with the gun shop, Pete opened Turkey Trot Acres and guided about a dozen or so hunters his first year in business.

Business grew rapidly, and today Pete's operation is well known to turkey hunters everywhere through television programs and print media coverage. A longtime member of the National Wild Turkey Federation and a former president of his local chapter, Pete is a devoted turkey hunter with a preference for fall hunting with dogs.

Pete Clare

John Byrne

When it comes to turkey hunting dogs, John Byrne is *the* man. I heard words to this effect from so many people that it must be true.

With his two sons, Byrne raises beef cattle on a Bedford County, Virginia, farm that has been in his family for several generations. But Byrne wasn't always a farmer or a breeder of turkey dogs.

"I went to Notre Dame, where I hoped to learn law," he says. "But my studies were interrupted by World War II, and I never finished. I wound up on the farm." You sense, though, that Byrne has no regrets about this turn of events.

In the rural South of his youth, the bobwhite quail was king, and Byrne was very much a part of that tradition. He was almost 30 when a friend took him on a fall turkey hunt, with the warning that turkey hunting would ruin him for other forms of the sport. The warning proved prophetic, and Byrne has been a turkey hunter ever since.

Turkey hunting dogs were a part of the hunting culture in

John Byrne

that part of Virginia, with many families developing their own carefully bred strains of dogs strictly for the pursuit of turkeys. Byrne set about methodically developing his own line-bred strain of turkey dogs from a mix of Plott hound, English pointer, and English setter. Known today as Appalachian Turkey Dogs, they are prized possessions for the few turkey hunters fortunate enough to own them.

Thanks to modern cryogenics and the ability to preserve and freeze semen, John's first Appalachian Turkey Dog continues to produce offspring to this day. Byrne is 76 years old and still turkey hunting.

At this writing, according to the National Wild Turkey Federation, fall turkey hunting with dogs is legal in California, Colorado, Hawaii, Maryland, Montana, Nebraska, Nevada, New Jersey, New York, North Dakota, Ohio, Oregon, Texas, Vermont, West Virginia, and Wyoming. At least one state, Kansas, is considering allowing it in the near future. To say that interest in this unique form of the sport is growing would be an understatement.

Gundog men—and I fancy myself one—tend to talk a lot about hunting instinct in dogs, the consensus being that the different breeds and the individuals within those breeds have varying instincts to varying degrees, and that the trainer's job is to bring these out, enhance them, and perhaps polish the dog's performance in some way. Retrieving, for instance, seems to be instinctive in many dogs. Why will almost any decent Lab take joy in fetching sticks from the time it's a pup? Pointers, with few exceptions, must be force-trained to retrieve, which is a long and laborious process, and not every dog so trained is going to perform the task cheerfully with head high. On the other hand, pointers excel at putting their noses into the wind and scenting birds, while any beagle worth a dime, assuming the right environment, will soon have its nose to the ground tracking anything that leaves a scent, baying all the while.

Sometimes, of course, we ask dogs to do things that run counter to their instinct. My Brittany, Chester—curled up at my feet as I write these words—is a natural retriever. He delighted me by picking up the first cock pheasant I shot over him and bringing it cheerfully to my hand. I had a heck of a time making that dog staunch on point, though, and even today, when the rooster he's pointing ducks out of the hedge and hotfoots it down a corn row, every fiber of Chester's quivering body suggests to me that his instinct is to run after that bird *right now.* We're still working on those running birds, because now and again the instinct to give chase overwhelms the training to remain motionless.

What fascinates me about turkey hunting dogs is that so much of what they're asked to do would seem to require an unusual mix of instinctive behaviors. They must not only find turkeys and scatter them but also stay in the general area from which the birds were scattered, and announce their find to hunters by barking until the hunters arrive on the scene. They must be independent enough to cover a lot of ground in their search, but not so independent that they run off into the next county and themselves become the object of the search. They must put the birds to flight but not chase them for any real distance. And they must do all these things reliably while out of the sight and any direct control of their handlers. What's more amazing, after they've scattered the birds and the hunters have arrived on the scene, they must sit or lie quietly enough to allow the birds to regroup and give the hunters an opportunity to call them into range and get off a good shot. Dogs that succeed at this style of turkey hunting must be very special dogs indeed.

Small wonder that most turkey dogs seem to be of mixed origins—a cross of hounds, bird dogs, spaniels, and curs. On the other hand, Boykin spaniels are often used as turkey dogs, and I'm aware of at least one breeder who bills his Labs as good turkey dogs.

As an avid turkey hunter who has always owned gundogs, I was chock-full of questions about the subject. What kind of dogs make good turkey hunting dogs? How much training is required, and how do you go about it? What's the most difficult thing for turkey hunting dogs to learn? Do turkey hunting dogs recover cripples? Retrieve them? How does using a turkey hunting dog change hunting strategies?

The enjoyment that turkey hunters experience in talking about their favorite sport is rivaled perhaps only by the enjoyment gundog owners experience in bragging about their dogs. I suppose it's not surprising, then, that the experts I spoke with responded so enthusiastically to my questions. They're all high on turkey hunting, and all seem to feel that adding dogs to the equation enhances an already exciting sport.

"It's a good sign you're not laughing," begins Gerry Bethge in response to my questions about turkey hunting with dogs. "Most people I mention it to laugh first and then ask a lot of questions."

A proud owner of one of John Byrne's line of famous Appalachian Turkey Dogs, Gerry is convinced that, while many dogs will chase and scatter a flock of turkeys, not just any dog can be used effectively on the big birds.

Good turkey dogs, according to Gerry, ". . . have stamina, speed, and can truly track ground scent like a Plott. I think this is what sets the Byrne line apart from the other lines of turkey dogs, of which there are quite a few. The absolute key to a turkey dog is its ability to bark on the flush, and this is where nonspecific turkey dogs typically fail. Because it's essential that these dogs range well, it's equally essential that they bark so that you're able to find and set up on the break site. . . . To my knowledge, this behavior is completely instinctual and cannot be taught."

In fact, Gerry is of the opinion that almost all of the turkey dog's behavior is instinctive, the notable exception being blind breaking, or teaching the dog to lie quietly as the scattered turkeys are called in.

"The only real form of training I've done with my dog are basic commands (more for use at home than in the woods), and blind breaking. He checks back consistently (I've never had to hunt him down in the five years I've hunted him), and all I've done is give him access to birds. The rest he's done on his own."

Gerry clarifies the role of the dog in remaining at the break site and barking until hunters arrive.

"The dogs don't so much remain at the break site waiting for your arrival," he explains, "as they work the break site area in search of runners, or birds that haven't yet taken wing, preferring to run off to escape danger. The key to a good break is to get the birds as separated as possible, and a dog does this far better than a hunter on foot could ever do."

Dogs are dogs, of course, and not even the best of them perform with machinelike consistency. Gerry concedes that his turkey dog could use a little polishing when it comes to remaining still in the blind.

"I find that my dog's ability to lie still is directly related to the amount of running he's done to break the flock. If he busts birds right off the bat in the A.M., he's fidgety in the blind. Later in the day, or if we have a dead bird in the blind with us, you never even know he's there. When someone shoots, however, he's immediately up and out of the blind."

In response to a question about recovering wounded turkeys with dogs, Gerry responds enthusiastically.

"You're correct—using dogs greatly increases the recovery rate. My favorite dog story took place a couple of years ago when a hunting buddy crippled a hen. Typically, I set up the blind 75 yards or so from the hunter with the gun. I had two guys with me, and after the first one shot, we sat still in the hope of taking another bird. After the birds quieted down, the dog and I headed over to my buddy, who was downcast and shaking his head. He had hit a bird, but it gotten up and walked away. Because I told him to sit tight after the shot, he didn't come and get me, wasting valuable scenting conditions. It was almost an hour after he shot that I pointed Jake in the cripple's direction. He got birdy almost immediately. I looked up to see a bird pop up from under a blowdown with Jake hot on its tail feathers. I called to the other hunters not to shoot amid the confusion and looked up to see Jake happily trotting toward me, tail wagging madly, with a very-much-alive turkey in his mouth. He brought it to hand!

"This year he found a bird I had crippled that managed to fly. He visually tracked it through the air and headed off after it. It tumbled from a tree and he pinned it to the ground. So as you can see, they're invaluable for finding crips."

Bethge's favorite tactic for fall turkeys, and one that he feels is made even more effective by the use of dogs, is to scatter birds right before fly-up time in the evening, for the next morning's hunt.

"Jake busted a flock of 20-plus birds feeding in a clover field late one afternoon. Birds scattered in all directions. We arrived at the break site almost an hour before sunrise, set out the decoys, and waited for first light. It was slow in coming, but the birds were raucous—gobbling, kee-kees, yelping, gobbler yelping. It was an awesome morning hunt. . . . We ended up with one kill and three misses!"

Pete Clare owns and operates Turkey Trot Acres in upstate New York. There are no guarantees when it comes to hunting wild turkeys, especially when clients book a typical three-day hunt. Nonetheless, paying customers expect high success rates, and Pete is convinced his turkey dogs contribute greatly to the consistent success of his fall turkey hunting operation. Late in the season, when birds are educated, or anytime hunting conditions are tough, Pete feels that dogs can tip the odds in the right direction.

Hunting turkeys with dogs, and even the shooting of hens and young-of-the-year turkeys in the fall, is controversial in some areas, but Pete's experience over the years with fall and spring turkey hunting at Turkey Trot Acres has led him to some interesting observations.

"I think our fall turkey hunting is one reason we have great gobbler hunting in the spring," Clare insists. He compares taking hens in the fall to shooting does.

"If you take only gobblers from an area," he points out, "you end up with a population that's out of balance. You have a lot more hens than gobblers. The same way you'll take more big bucks if the buck-to-doe ratio is high and the bucks must compete more for does, you'll take more gobblers if they must compete more for the available hens."

Pete dismisses the idea that taking a limited number of hens from an area will adversely affect the population, citing Lovett Williams's studies about carrying capacity.

"A given area can only support so many turkeys. What happens when it reaches the carrying capacity is that a higher proportion of hens become barren—they just don't nest and reproduce."

Pete relates this back to improved gobbler hunting, theorizing that barren hens will spend more time with gobblers, never leaving them to nest, and hence making the gobblers much less responsive to calling.

"Besides," he continues, "turkeys are too smart to succumb to ethical hunting. They get educated in a hurry. We have 60,000 acres to hunt here, but in the unlikely event we think we've hunted the same flock five or six times, we leave it alone. This is partly a conservation measure, but it's also because those birds get too hard to hunt, even with the dogs."

Pete emphasizes that while dogs add a lot to the hunt and give hunters an extra edge, hunting with dogs is still turkey hunting, and still challenging.

"Woodsmanship is still important," he says. "There's still the matter of calling—when to call and when not to, how to call, where to set up, and all the rest of it.

"Often when the birds scatter, a few of them will fly over you, so you know what you're hunting," Pete continues. "But when they don't, you don't know whether you're hunting a family flock, a group of hens, or a few mature gobblers. So you don't know how to call to them. You don't want to be doing kee-kees to gobblers. You usually have to wait until you hear the birds calling to figure out what they are so you'll know what strategy to use."

Pete points out several situations that present special challenges.

"Hunting when the woods are dry is really tough," he says. "Scenting conditions are not good, but the real problem is the noise. Turkeys can hear you—and the dogs—from 300 yards away. They're alert, they're moving, and it's really tough for the dogs to get a good break and scatter the turkeys. They just fly off together as a flock, and then they're almost impossible to call in."

The heavy foliage of early autumn can make for tough conditions, too.

"The birds are a lot less vocal in heavy foliage," says Pete. "They just don't call as much. Also, sometimes in heavy foliage the birds will just fly up into nearby trees and not budge. They won't call and they won't move, and there's not much you can do.

"When we see birds in a field," Pete says, turning to specific strategies, "that can be difficult. The dogs can't scatter them properly when the turkeys see them coming. Ideally, you want to wait until the birds have moved into the woods at least a couple of hundred yards, then try to work the dogs toward them."

Another challenge occurs when a flock has been scattered and the hen comes back and begins calling loudly.

"The issue then is whether or not to release the dogs to break the flock up again. If you don't, the other birds will probably get back with the hen quickly and move off. Sometimes we have to bust up a flock three or four times to get in position for some shooting."

Many hunters using dogs wait until later in the morning to begin hunting, so turkeys will have spent some time leaving scent on the ground. Pete has discovered another reason to hunt later in his area.

"There are a lot of ridges around here, and the turkeys often roost on the ridges," he explains. "If we're out early and flush birds off those ridges, they'll often pitch off and fly out over the valley 700 yards or so, and we'll never see them again. By going later in the morning, we're more likely to catch them in level country where we can get a good break. Getting a 360-degree break is the whole secret to fall turkey hunting."

One mistake hunters often make, according to Pete, is to leave the breakup spot. Hunters often see a few birds going in a certain direction and succumb to the temptation to move 100 or 200 yards in this direction to set up. Inevitably, the turkeys end up regrouping at the break site the hunters have just left.

Finally, Pete likes to point out that hunting with dogs is an ideal way to introduce newcomers to turkey hunting. Spring turkey hunting can be great for newcomers on days when there's plenty of action and hunters see birds, but those difficult days when birds aren't vocal and action is slow can be particularly boring to the new turkey hunter.

"In fall," asserts Pete, "there's almost always some action. Sooner or later we will find a flock. It might take six hours, but we'll find them, and it will be exciting. Turkey hunters get pumped up on fall birds, and when they get a turkey, they feel they've earned it.

"Turkey hunting in the fall is very different," he says, "but it's still turkey hunting."

"Going turkey hunting without a dog," says John Byrne, in a soft Virginia drawl, "is like going on a honeymoon without a bride. It just ain't the same."

Producing the line-bred strain of famous Appalachian Turkey Dogs was a labor of love for John.

"Whatever money there is in breeding dogs," he says, "is still in there. I didn't get none of it out."

John has looked into registering his dogs with a club that would acknowledge them as a recognized breed, but ran into two problems. First, there are relatively few Appalachian Turkey Dogs in existence. Second, registering the dogs would result in some loss of control over the strain, since other breeders would inevitably experiment with their own breeding programs. That, in John's words, ". . . would be like cutting fine wine with water."

The story of how John developed his line of turkey dogs is instructive, since it reveals something about the qualities that are important in these dogs. The stimulus to develop his very own line of turkey dogs was simple: Good turkey dogs were hard to come by. Local families who had good ones guarded them jealously. In some cases they would make pups available to family members only; any surplus dogs were put down.

"The Appalachian Turkey Dog," says John, "came out of a hound and a bunch of nondescript, discarded bird dogs. I found a Plott hound that barked at turkeys, and bred her to a pointer. Then I found an English setter. That dog was from field-trial stock, but when she found birds she would walk in stiff-legged and bark at them, so the owner wasn't too happy with the dog. 'That's the dog I want,' I said. I bred that dog to my half hound, half pointer, and in that litter was Junior, the first Appalachian Turkey Dog."

The barking is key, according to John.

"A dog that won't bark is worse than no dog at all. It just spooks birds and chases them away."

Important as barking is, ideally a turkey dog will hunt and trail silently, barking only upon surprising the turkeys. Otherwise, the birds will run off or fly off together, instead of scattering. In many cases this is simply a matter of experience. Pups that get excited and bark on the trail often learn better very quickly.

John developed the bag that's now commonly used by many turkey hunters after watching dogs shiver in cold weather. Many of the traits exhibited by good turkey dogs seem to be inherent or instinctive, but lying quietly in a blind or bag is purely a matter of training.

"When it comes to training a dog," explains John, "there's a magic eight weeks when the dog is between eight and sixteen weeks old. That's when it learns fastest.

"I sit in the yard and let my puppies be puppies. I get them in my lap and stroke them and say 'stay' real firm. I hold them gently, and when I can count to five I'll say 'stay' again, maintaining light pressure. On a count of four I'll release them. The trick is, you never release the dog when it wants to go—only when it's lying still and you're ready to release it. Pretty soon they'll lie quietly and even go to sleep when I tell them to stay."

John introduces the dogs to the bags early on, as well, letting them play with the bags and lie on them. He makes a game of putting the bags over the dogs and encouraging the dogs to climb into the bags so that getting into them becomes fun.

"I detest the term *blind breaking* by the way," he says. "To me, a dog that's 'broken' is a dog that has something wrong with it. I much prefer *blind training*.

"I need to reemphasize that a turkey dog needs to be of trainable quality. It should be a dog that will rage through the woods like a maniac looking for turkeys, then lie down quietly on command after it's found them."

The key to success, as John explains it, is to modify a dog's predatory instincts just enough, but not too much.

"I sent a pup to an obedience school once," he notes. "They kept him four months. When he came back he would heel, fetch, sit, and stay. He wouldn't hunt, though. He just wanted to stay with me and be obedient all the time."

The independence to range wide is another quality for a good turkey dog.

"If it hunts close," insists John, "it'll miss birds."

Finally, John has a bit of folk wisdom to share about spring turkey hunting.

"About the most low-down thing a man can do," he muses, "is to gobbler hunt in the spring. A hunter who does that is taking unfair advantage of an inclination that has brought down many a good man. Jim Baker is one. Mike Tyson comes to mind. You remember that Gary Hart fella, he was another one. I think the last occupant of the White House had a little trouble along those lines, too."

The man has a point.

Wild Turkey Recipes

With few exceptions, the meat of wild game is superior in every way to that of domestic animals—more healthful and better tasting. Okay, so that's a minority opinion. It's an informed opinion, though, and one that's shared by hunters, gourmet chefs, and epicures the world over.

Debatable as the quality of some wild game may be, at least among those who think food comes from grocery stores, few who have tasted it will argue the quality of wild turkey. The breast of wild turkey might not in every case be as finely textured, or as white, as that of its domestic counterparts, but it's every bit as tender and is even more flavorful.

As with all wild game, proper care begins in the field. In many cases, simply hanging the bird by one leg in the shade will cool it considerably. In particularly warm weather, or in a case where a turkey cannot be thoroughly cleaned and put on ice, refrigerated, or frozen within three hours or so, it's probably a good idea to field-dress it by carefully opening it between the vent and sternum and removing the entrails. Some hunters go a step farther and remove the crop, but I'm not convinced this is necessary. I've never done it, and with the exception of one or two birds that were overcooked, every wild turkey I've eaten has been delicious.

A turkey may be plucked, which is preferred if the plan is to bake it or roast it whole. If it's going to be fried—an excellent and nearly foolproof way to prepare a wild turkey—don't bother with plucking. Just skin the bird out, which is much faster and easier; then remove the breasts, cutting them into strips or nuggets if you prefer. (The exception is if you are going to deep-fry the bird whole.) Legs may be used for soup, stew, or gravy stock. Don't even think about eating them baked— they're far too tough, except possibly in the case of juvenile birds taken in the fall.

Dry plucking is a chore. Turkeys can be plucked by dipping them into very hot water. The downside of this is that it takes a little practice to do it efficiently. If the water isn't hot enough, it doesn't work. If the water is too hot, or the bird is exposed to the hot water too long, the skin cooks, then tears. Many hunters put the bird in a tub and use a large dipper or ladle to pour measured amounts of hot water over the turkey. This allows them to experiment a little, using more hot water as necessary. Once the technique is mastered, however, it's much easier than dry plucking. It simply takes practice on a few birds to develop the knack.

Wild turkey should be prepared in the same way as domestic turkey, but two things should be kept in mind. First, wild turkeys are not as round as domestic ones, which means the baking or roasting time is usually a little shorter. Second, wild turkeys aren't Butterballs. They lack the fat of domestic birds; nor have they been prebasted or injected with fats or oils, as is the case with some grocery-store turkeys. When roasted, they require just a little more attention than do most domestic turkeys. Basting regularly with butter, white wine, pan drippings, or fruit juices is a good idea. Some cooks pin bacon strips to the breast. I have soaked cheesecloth in wine and pan drippings, then covered the breast with these until time for browning the bird. This works well, so long as you don't let the cheesecloth dry out and catch fire. I've also simply kept the turkey covered in a large roasting pan, or kept aluminum foil over it, and this too can help keep it juicy.

Any recipe created with domestic turkeys in mind should work equally well for wild turkey. Here are a few of my own favorites.

SEASONED ROAST TURKEY

The first recipe is a simple one. The paste helps season the bird and keep it moist while contributing to an even, golden brown color.

1 turkey	¼ cup flour
1 lemon	salt and pepper
½ cup vegetable oil	2–4 apples, sliced
⅓ cup butter or margarine, melted	½ cup chopped celery

Juice the lemon and combine the juice with the oil.

Mix the melted butter and flour into the paste, adding salt, pepper, and any additional desired seasonings to taste. Spread the paste over the outside of the turkey.

Stuff the turkey with the apples and celery, and tie the turkey up. Bake at 325°F for approximately 4 hours or until tender.

Baste frequently with the oil and lemon mix and pan juices.

FRIED TURKEY

Here's a quick, basic fried turkey recipe that's hard to beat.

1 skinned turkey	salt and pepper
2 cups milk	Cajun spice mix
2 cups flour	1 quart oil (preferably peanut oil)

Breast out the turkey, remove the thigh meat from the bones, and cut it into bite-sized cubes. Dip the cubes in the milk and roll in a mix of the flour, salt and pepper, and any commercially available Cajun spice mix. Fry in hot oil until golden brown.

WILD TURKEY RICE SOUP

It's a shame to waste the meat on a turkey's legs and back, not to mention all the little scraps that are invariably left on the bird after the bigger pieces are removed for leftovers. This recipe leaves nothing to waste.

1 turkey	½ teaspoon thyme
Approximately 10 cups water	pinch of parsley
1 bay leaf	salt and pepper
2 carrots, chopped	5 cups cooked wild rice

Break up the carcass and put it in a pot with the water; bring to a boil. Add all ingredients except the rice. Simmer for about 2 hours.

Remove the carcass, pulling off any remaining meat to put back in the soup. Skim any excess fat, add the rice, and simmer for 20 to 30 minutes.

PAN TURKEY AND MORELS

It's a happy coincidence that spring turkey season is also spring mushroom season in much of the United States. I contacted nationally renowned mushroom expert Larry Lonik for a few tips on turkeys and mushrooms. His first suggestion: Toss 10 or 12 morels into the pan with a cup of water for the last hour of baking to make a great gravy. The recipe below is adapted from Lonik's book *Basically Morels*. See www.morelheaven.com for additional morel recipes.

3 pounds large turkey pieces	4 cups heavy cream
Seasoned flour	1 large egg yolk
¼ cup butter	Salt

2 tablespoons oil   Freshly ground black
⅓ cup dry white wine   pepper
1½ pounds morels, cleaned, sliced   Lemon juice (optional)

Dredge the turkey in seasoned flour and brown lightly in the butter and oil. A sauté pan of at least 14 inches would be preferable. Add the wine and cook until the wine is almost evaporated, turning the turkey occasionally. Add the morels and cream and cook, uncovered, until the turkey is done. Remove, with as many morels as possible, to a hot serving dish. Boil down the sauce by half, and thicken by beating the egg yolk with a little of the sauce, then cooking it all together for about 5 minutes. Season to taste with salt and pepper. Lemon juice may be added. Pour over the turkey and serve. Rice goes well with this dish.

TURKEY POT PIE

Something about the often cool, wet weather of spring reminds me of the hot and hearty chicken potpies that were a staple in my family when I was a kid. Here's a recipe for something even better: turkey potpie.

2 cups cubed turkey   ⅔ cup milk
⅓ cup butter or margarine   1¾ cups chicken or turkey broth
⅓ cup chopped onion   1 package frozen peas and
⅓ cup flour   carrots
Salt and pepper   Pastry shell (below)

Melt the butter over low heat, then blend in the onion, flour, salt, and pepper. Stir over low heat; remove from the heat when mixture is smooth and simmering. Stir in the milk and broth. Bring to a boil while stirring. Add the turkey and frozen vegetables.

Roll two-thirds of the pastry into a 13-inch square, and put this into a square 9×9×2 inch pan. Pour the turkey mixture into the pan. Roll the rest of the pastry into an 11-inch square and put this over the filling. Roll or decorate the edges and cut slits in the center of the pie top. Cook uncovered at 425° until the crust is brown, 30 to 40 minutes. Serves 6.

Pastry

⅔ cup shortening   1 teaspoon salt
2 cups flour   ¼ cup water

Cut the shortening into the flour and salt. Dribble the water onto flour, mixing with a fork, then roll the mixture into a ball. (Add water if necessary before rolling into a ball.)

TURKEY CAMP STEW

On a memorable hunt in Tennessee, four of us filled tags on opening day. The cabin was comfortable but lacked refrigerator space for that many birds. It also lacked spices, stuffing ingredients, sauces, and garnishes. No problem. We used the recipe below, and served the stew with biscuits and cold beer on a cool, rainy evening for a meal that was almost as memorable as the hunt.

1 wild turkey, skinned   salt
1 large onion, sliced   pepper
1–2 cups chopped celery   parsley (optional)
2 sliced carrots

Breast out the turkey, remove the thigh meat, and cut the turkey into large, bite-sized pieces. Place the meat (along with the neck and giblets, if desired) into a large pan or kettle, adding just enough water to cover the meat. Add the remaining ingredients, along with (if desired) potato cubes, tomato wedges, sliced green peppers, or what have you. Heat to boiling, then reduce the heat to a simmer and cover. Cook until all the meat is tender, probably 3 hours or more.

TURKEY SALAD WITH CELERY AND GRAPES

If you like chicken salad, you'll love turkey salad. Here's a classic recipe.

3 cups roasted or poached turkey in small bite-sized pieces
½ cup mayonnaise
½ cup sour cream
1 cup chopped celery

¾ cups white grapes, cut in half
watercress, lettuce (Bibb or Boston), or chicory

Mix the mayonnaise and sour cream. (Or use all mayonnaise if you prefer.) Mix the chicken and mayonnaise, sour cream with the celery, and grapes. Arrange the mixture on bed of watercress, lettuce, or chicory. For a classy touch, garnish with toasted almonds.

STIR-FRIED TURKEY AND PINEAPPLE

The next one is among my long-time favorite recipes, adapted over the years from a recipe designed for a smaller, more common, less interesting domestic fowl. A large wok works best for this, but in a pinch I've done it in large frying pans—and it came out fine. Quantities of the ingredients need not be exact. Experiment, using more or less of each to suit your taste.

1 skinned turkey breast
2 tablespoons plus two teaspoons soy sauce
2 tablespoons plus two teaspoons cornstarch
1 teaspoon salt

½ garlic clove
¼ cup water
2 teaspoons vinegar
½ cup pineapple juice
6–8 tablespoons oil
8 slices canned pineapple

Cut the turkey into bite-sized pieces. Combine 2 teaspoons of the soy sauce with 2 teaspoons of the cornstarch and the salt. Add this to the turkey and coat. Cut the pineapple slices into 5 or 6 pieces each.

Mince the garlic and combine it with the rest of the corn-starch and soy sauce, along with the water, vinegar, and pine-apple juice.

Heat the oil and add the turkey. Stir-fry until almost brown, then add the pineapple pieces and cook, covered, over low heat for 4 minutes or so, then remove to a serving dish.

Pour the garlic-cornstarch sauce into a wok and stir over low-to-medium heat until thick. Pour over the turkey and the pineapple pieces and serve.

CURRIED TURKEY WITH GRAPEFRUIT

And now for something totally different (but good) . . .

2–3 pounds skinned turkey breast
½ cup water
1½ cups vegetable juice cocktail
1 chicken bouillon cube
½ cup chopped onion
1 teaspoon curry powder

½ teaspoon poultry
  seasoning
½ teaspoon salt
pepper
1 tablespoon flour
8½-ounce can grapefruit
  sections, drained

Combine the water, ½ cup of the vegetable juice cocktail, and the crushed chicken bouillon cube in a large skillet. Cut the turkey into large strips or pieces and put them in the skillet, adding the onion, curry powder, poultry seasoning, salt, and pepper. Simmer, covered, for 45 to 55 minutes. Remove the turkey and skim the fat.

Stir the flour into the remaining vegetable juice cocktail, then pour into the skillet, stirring until thick. Put the turkey back into the sauce and top with the grapefruit sections, drained. Cover to heat, and serve. Serves 4.

Index

A
ACC shafts
    bowhunting, 78
Aerial photographs
    scouting, 18
Afternoon delight, 141–146
Age
    hunting tactics, 40
    turkey hunting, 142
Aggressive calling, 32, 101
    less
        later in season, 36
Aggressive hunting, 32
    Bent Creek, 38
Aggressive tactics
    early in seasons, 35
Aggressive turkey hunters, 33
All-day states
    vs. morning-only states, 142
American Wild Turkey, 9, 159
Anthropology professor
    John McDaniel, 9
Appalachian Turkey Dogs, 165, 174

B
Basically Morels, 180
Beginning turkey hunters
    blinds, 62
Behavior observations
    scouting, 27

Bent Creek Lodge
aggressive hunting, 38
Larry Norton, 11
Bethge, Gerry, 163–164
fall turkey, 170
picture, 163
turkey dogs, 168–169
Binoculars. *See also* Optics
Eddie Salter, 90
Peter Fiduccia, 91
reason, 86–88
scouting, 95
Blinds, 59–70
beginning turkey hunters, 62
bowhunting, 80, 82–83
calls, 70
friction, 63, 70
quietly, 64–65
camera, 67, 70
camo fabric, 67
camo netting, 61
characteristics, 65
clucks, 70
cylindrical
picture, 68
dark interiors, 66
decoys, 65, 69, 70
Dick Kirby, 65
dog breaking, 176
field-edge setups, 68
hunter comfort, 46, 59–61
kids, 62
Lovett Williams, 67
Matt Morrett, 67–68
natural, 63, 67
materials, 65
observing, 67
photographing, 67, 70
picture, 60
cylindrical, 68
portable, 73, 74
practice, 64
purrs, 61, 70
recording, 67
Roger Raisch, 68–70
scratch box, 61
shield-type camo, 69
Tim Hooey, 63–64
training, 176
whines, 70
youngsters, 61–63
Blizzard. *See also* Poor weather conditions
gobbling activity, 42
Boat paddle box calls, 109
Boat-paddle-style box calls, 35
Boots. *See also* Gear
hunter comfort, 43–45
Bow Grand Slam, 7–8, 136
Bowhunting, 63
Eddie Salter, 14

turkeys, 71–84
without blind, 72
Bow-killed turkey
picture, 60
Box calls, 127. *See also* Calling
boat paddle, 109
boat-paddle-style, 35
Eddie Salter, 13, 100
Breakup spot, 173
Breeding dogs
turkey dogs, 174
Broadheads. *See* Mechanical broadheads
Bumping, 104, 125
Bushnell. *See also* Optics
optical accessories, 88
Butski, Paul, 5–6
afternoon hunting, 144
last-ditch situations, 160–161
optics, 92
picture, 5
scouting, 25–26
setting up on turkeys, 114–116
Butski's Squirrel Game Calls, 5
Byrne, John, 165–166
picture, 165
turkey dogs, 174

C
Cabbage palms, 67
Calling, 118–120. *See also* Box calls; Locator calls; Mouth calls; Slate calls
aggressive, 32, 36, 101
blinds, 63–65, 70
championships
Paul Butski, 5
competitive
reasons, 105
crow calls, 101
Dick Kirby, 8, 109–110
Eddie Salter, 100–101
fall turkey hunting, 149, 152
frenetic, 31
friction, 10
gobblers
vulnerable to calling, 52
hawk calls, 101
high-volume, 35
Larry Norton, 11, 101–105
Lovett Williams, 108–109
Matt Morrett, 10, 109
owl calls, 101
pileated woodpecker calls, 101
poor weather hunting, 45–46
Quaker Boy Game Calls, 8
quietly, 64–65
rainy weather, 49
regularly, 35
Richard Combs, 99
role in turkey hunting, 98
scouting
pros and cons, 24–25

Calling (*continued*)
    secrets, 97–110
    soft reassuring, 55
    Tim Hooey, 105–108
    turkey calling championships
        Paul Butski, 5
    turkey dogs, 172
Camera. *See also* Photographing
    blinds, 70
Camo fabric
    blinds, 67
Camo netting
    blinds, 61
Challenging dominant hens, 31
Clare, Pete
    picture, 164
    turkey dogs, 170–174
Closeness, 111–120
Clothing. *See also* Gear
    slam hunting, 138
Clucking, 127. *See also* Calling
    blinds, 70
    fall turkey hunting, 149
    henned-up gobblers, 56
Cold temperatures. *See also* Poor weather conditions
    hunt effectively, 42
    hunting tactics, 36
    turkey hunting, 47
Combs, Richard
    calling, 99
    picture, 3, 60, 95, 133
Comfort. *See also* Hunter comfort
    hunting tactics, 43
Compass
    scouting as he hunts, 69
Competitive turkey calling
    reasons, 105
Creek bottom
    scouting, 24
Cross, Tom
    silent woods, 122
Crow calls, 101
Curried turkey
    recipe, 184
Cylindrical blind
    Roger Raisch
        picture, 68

D
Decoys, 120
    blinds, 65, 69, 70
    bowhunting, 78–80, 83
    hen, 80
    henned-up gobblers, 56
    jake, 80
    picture, 84
    pros and cons, 95
Deer hunter
    Eddie Salter, 14

Peter Fiduccia, 6
Roger Raisch, 13
Dogs. *See also* Turkey dogs
    Appalachian Turkey, 165, 174
    barking, 175
    blind breaking or training, 176
    turkey hunting, 91
    for turkey hunting, 163–176
Dominant hen
    challenging, 103
Downhill, 111–120
Draw weight
    bowhunting, 78–80
Droppings
    signs, 20, 21
Dry plucking, 178
Dusting area
    signs, 20, 28

E
Eastern turkeys, 137, 138
    picture, 2
Eddie Salter box call, 13, 100
Educating turkeys
    run and gun, 36–37
    warning, 20, 24–26, 36
    worry, 55
Electronic TrackMaster
    bowhunting, 80–81
Elevation
    hunting tactics, 138, 140
    slam hunting, 140
English setter pointer
    turkey dogs, 174–175
Ethical issue, 157

F
Fall turkey hunting, 22, 27, 147–152
    calling, 149, 152
    clucks, 149
    Dick Kirby, 149–150
    with dogs
        legal, 166
    Gerry Bethge, 170
    locating flocks, 158
    Matt Morrett, 149
    Roger Raisch, 150–152
    scattering family flocks, 148
    turkey dogs
        legal with dogs, 166
    yelps, 149
Feathers
    signs, 20, 21
Feeding areas
    henned-up gobblers, 56
    signs, 20
Fiduccia, Kate
    with gobbler
        picture, 96

Fiduccia, Peter, 6–7
    binoculars, 91
    optics, 91–92
    picture, 6
    poor weather hunting, 49
    scouting, 24–25
    silent woods, 127
Field-edge setups
    blinds, 68
Filming. *See also* Photographing
    Lovett Williams, 14
Finger shooter
    bowhunting setup, 80–82
Fog. *See also* Poor weather conditions
    roost, 49
4 day hunt, 141–142
Frenetic calling, 31
Frequent relocating, 31, 32, 120
Friction call, 10
    blinds, 63, 70

G
Game calling. *See also* Calling
    Dick Kirby, 8
Game Tracker, 80–82
Game wardens
    scouting, 19
Gang of turkeys, 58
Gear, 43–45, 67. *See also* Hunter comfort
    slam hunting, 138
Ghillie suits, 67
Glassing, 22
Gobblers. *See also* Turkeys
    hang up, 120
    track sign
        picture, 23
    vulnerable to calling, 52
    yelp, 150
Gobbling turkey
    activity
        blizzard, 42
        snow squalls, 42
    hunter position, 111–120
    periods, 52–54
    setup, 111-120
Gould's turkeys, 67
    Mexican, 130
    picture, 131
Grand Slam. *See also* Slams
    with bow, 7–8, 136
    defined, 130
    Dick Kirby, 132–134
Ground
    covering style, 35
    familiar, 17
Gundog men, 166

H
Ham Slam, 129

Harvest statistics, 123
    scouting, 19
Hawk calls, 101
Hen decoys. *See also* Decoys
    bowhunters, 80
Henned-up gobblers
    hunting, 51–58
    pattern gobblers, 56
Henned-up tom
    hunting, 54–55
Hide, 63, 67
Hide-N-Pine camouflage, 6
High-pitched kee-kee, 151
High visibility setups
    hunting tactics, 38–39
High-volume calls, 35
High winds. *See also* Poor weather conditions
    John McDaniel, 49
Holographic scopes
    Larry Norton, 96
Holographic sighting device, 88
Hooey, Tim, 7–8, 126–127
    bowhunting setup, 75–77
    calling skills, 105–108
    Grand Slam, 136
      with bow, 7
    henned-up gobblers, 56–57
    locator calls, 106
    picture, 7
    wait 'em out, 64–65
Hot seat
    hunter comfort, 50
Hot-weather experience
    Roger Raisch, 48
Hunter comfort
    blinds, 46, 59–61
    boots, 43–45
    gear, 43–45
    hot seat, 50
    layering, 43
    rain gear, 43
Hunters
    beginning
      blinds, 62
Hunter's Specialties
    Matt Morrett, 10
Hunting
    4 day hunt, 141–142
    outfitter
      selection, 134
      successful hunt, 135–136
    states
      all-day *vs.* morning-only, 142
Hunting blinds. *See* Blinds
Hunting slams. *See* Slams
Hunting tactics
    age, 40
    aggressive tactics
      early in seasons, 35

Hunting tactics (*continued*)
    cold temperatures, 36
    comfort, 43
    elevation, 138, 140
    factors affect, 20
    high visibility setups, 38–39
    last-ditch tactics, 153–162
        John McDaniel, 159
        Larry Norton, 161
        Lovett Williams, 158
        Steve Puppe, 155–156
    leapfrog, 35
    patience, 32
    persistence, 39
    physical condition, 40
    vs. terrain, 134
    various strategies, 3–4
    weather, 36
    windy days, 35–36

I
Impatient hunters, 33
Internet resources
    scouting, 19

J
Jakes, 58, 159–160
    decoys
        bowhunters, 80

K
Kee-kee
    high-pitched, 151
Kids
    blinds, 61–63
Kirby, Dick, 8–9
    blinds, 65
    bowhunting setup, 77–80
    calling, 109–110
    fall turkey hunting, 149–150
    Grand Slams, 132–134
    picture, 8
    setting up, 117–118
    wait 'em out, 35

L
Laser rangefinder, 90, 94. *See also* Optics
    optical accessories, 88
    picture, 89
Last-ditch tactics, 153–162
Layering
    hunter comfort, 43
Lay of the land
    importance of, 17
Leapfrog hunting tactic, 35
Leica. *See also* Optics
    optical accessories, 88
Less aggressive calling
    later in season, 36

Local residents
    scouting, 19
Location, 111–120
Locator calls, 28, 101, 104, 121. *See also* Calling
    Larry Norton, 104
    Tim Hooey, 106
    volume, 101
Logging roads
    scouting, 19, 24
Lonik, Larry, 180

M
Mathews Conquest, 75
Mathews single cam
    bowhunting setup, 80–82
Mathews SQ2 bow, 82–83
McDaniel, John, 9–10
    henned-up gobblers, 55
    henned-up toms, 55
    high winds, 49
    last-ditch tactics, 159
    optics, 90–91
    picture, 9
    poor weather hunting, 49
    scouting, 20–22
    silent woods, 126
Mechanical broadheads, 73, 77
    bowhunting, 82
        NAP's, 78
    picture, 82
Merriam's gobblers, 106, 136, 138
    picture, 112
        scouting, 137
Methods. *See* Hunting tactics
Mexican Gould's turkey, 130
Minimum-impact scouting, 127
Morning-only states
    vs. all-day states, 142
Morrett, Matt, 10–11
    afternoon hunting, 146
    blinds, 67–68
    calling, 10, 109
    fall turkey hunting, 149
    favorite hunting place, 140
    picture, 10
    setup, 120
    silent woods, 128
Mouth calls, 127. *See also* Calling
    advantage, 110
    care of, 107
    cleaning of, 107
    modification, 107
    rainy weather, 49
    storage, 107
    three-or four-reed hand-stretched, 151
Moving, 128. *See also* Relocating

N
NAP Gobbler Getters
    bowhunting, 82

NAP's mechanical broadheads. *See* Mechanical broadheads
Natural blinds, 63, 67
Natural materials
    and blinds, 65
Nikon. *See also* Optics
    optical accessories, 88
North American Fish and Game
    television program, 7
Norton, Larry, 11–12
    afternoon hunting, 144–146
    bowhunting setup, 83–84
    calling style, 101–105
    henned-up gobblers, 54–55
    holographic or red-dot scopes, 96
    last-ditch tactic, 161
    locator calls, 104
    optics, 92–94
    picture, 11
    run and gun, 37–39
    setups, 118–120
    thunderstorms and rainy weather hunting, 46–47

O
Observing. *See also* Scouting
    blinds, 67
Ocellated turkey, 130
Optics. *See also* Binoculars; Laser rangefinder; Scopes
    turkey hunting, 85–96
Osceolas, 132, 137
    picture, 133
Outdoor Expeditions
    television programs, 12
Outdoorsman's Edge Book Club, 7
Outfitter
    selection, 134
    successful hunt, 135–136
Owl calls, 101
Owl Hooting Championships
    Paul Butski, 5

P
Patience
    henned-up gobblers, 56
    important virtue, 33
    later in season, 36
    tactic, 32
    turkey hunting, 160
Pattern
    shotgun, 92, 93
Pattern gobblers, 22, 27
    henned-up gobblers, 56
    scouting, 26, 56
Persistence
    hunting tactics, 39
Photographing
    aerial
        scouting, 18
    blinds, 67
    Lovett Williams, 14

Physical condition
    hunting tactics, 40
Pileated woodpecker calls, 101
Plat maps
    scouting, 18
Plott, 168, 174–175
Plucked, 178
Poor weather conditions
    calling, 45–46
    Eddie Salter, 45–46
    gobbling activity, 42
    gobbling periods, 52–54
    hunt effectively, 42
    hunting tactics, 36, 46
    importance of not giving up, 48
    John McDaniel, 49
    mouth calls, 49
    Peter Fiduccia, 49
    Roger Raisch, 47–49
    scouting, 45–46
    strut zone, 48–49
    turkeys movements, 47
Portable blinds, 73, 74
Positioning, 111–120
Puppe, Steve, 12
    bowhunting, 82–83
    favorite hunting place, 140
    henned-up gobblers, 57
    last-ditch tactics, 155–156
    picture, 12
    preparing for slam, 137–139
Purring, 127. See also Calling
    blinds, 61, 70
    henned-up gobblers, 56

Q
Quaker Boy Game Calls, 8

R
Rain gear. See also Gear
    hunter comfort, 43
Rainy weather
    gobbling periods, 52–54
    hunt effectively, 42
    mouth calls, 49
    turkeys movements, 47
Raisch, Roger, 12–13
    blinds, 68–70
    bowhunting setup, 80–82
    cylindrical blind
        picture, 68
    fall turkey hunting, 150–152
    picture, 13
    poor weather hunting, 47–49
    scouting, 27–29
Rangefinder
    optical accessories, 88
Recording
    blinds, 67

Red-dot, 88
   scopes
      Larry Norton, 96
      sights, 94
Relocating, 120, 128
   frequent, 31
   often, 32
Rio Grande gobbler, 132, 134, 136, 137
   picture, 3, 139
Roosting site, 146
   bumping, 104, 125
   fog, 49
   henned-up gobblers, 56, 57
   locate, 24
   rainy weather, 48
   signs, 20, 21
Royal Slam
   defined, 130
Run and gun
   vs. wait 'em out, 31–40

S
Safety issue, 157
Salter, Eddie, 13–14
   about calling, 100–101
   binoculars, 90
   optics, 88–90
   picture, 13
   poor hunting, 45–46
   run and gun, 33–34
   scouting, 22–23
   setting up on gobblers, 116–117
   silent woods, 125–126
Scattering family flocks
   fall turkey hunting, 148
Scents
   track ground, 168
Scopes, 88. *See also* Optics
   bowhunting setup, 80–82
   holographic
      Larry Norton, 96
   Peter Fiduccia, 91
   power recommended, 88
   red-dot sights, 94
   Tasco red-dot, 94
Scouting, 17–29
   aerial photographs, 18
   behavior observations, 27
   binoculars, 95
   bow-killed turkey, 95
   calls
      pros and cons, 24–25
   creek bottom, 24
   game wardens, 19
   harvest statistics, 19
   important aspect, 19–20
   Internet resources, 19
   John McDaniel, 20–22
   local residents, 19

logging roads, 19, 24
Lovett Williams, 26–27
Merriam's scouting, 137
minimum-impact, 127
new areas, 20–22
new turkey hunting spots, 25
pattern gobblers, 26
Paul Butski, 25–26
Peter Fiduccia, 24–25
poor weather hunting, 45–46
prior to season, 22, 24–25
purposes, 19
Roger Raisch, 27–29
Salter, Eddie, 22–23
seasonal, 27
spring turkey hunting, 51
spring vs. fall, 22
starting point, 24
strut zones, 29
topo and plat maps, 18
using optics, 88–90
while hunting, 69
wildlife biologists, 19
Scratching, 127
in leaves, 108
scratch box
blinds, 61
Tom Gaskins scratch box, 99–100
Seasonal scouting, 27
Seasoned roast turkey
recipe, 179–180
Shade, 111–120
Shellshucker, 72
Shield-type camo blind, 69
Sights
bowhunting, 78
holographic sighting device, 88
red-dot
scopes, 88, 94, 96
telescopic
advantage, 95–97
Silent woods, 121–128
Simulating gobbler fights, 31
Slams, 129–140
bow Grand Slam, 7–8, 136
defined, 130
Dick Kirby, 132–134
slam hunting, 129
clothing, 138
elevation, 140
Steve Puppe preparing, 137–139
Tim Hooey, 7, 136
Slate calls, 107, 109, 127. *See also* Calling
picture, 99
Sleep deprivation
turkey hunting, 142
Smokepole, 72
Snow. *See also* Poor weather conditions
hunt effectively, 42

Snow (*continued*)
 squalls
  gobbling activity, 42
  turkeys movements, 47
Soft yelps. *See* Yelps
Speed, 168
Spring turkey hunting, 20–22, 27, 51
 folk wisdom, 176
Stalk
 turkeys, 57
Stamina, 168
Stir-fried turkey
 recipe, 183-184
Strategies. *See* Hunting tactics
String trackers, 73, 77
Strong, Hank, 129
Strutting
 picture, 143
 signs, 20
Strut zones
 henned-up gobblers, 56
 poor weather hunting, 48–49
 scouting, 29
Sunlight, 111–120
Swamp buggies
 Florida turkeys, 138
Swarovski
 optics, 90

T
Tactics. *See* Hunting tactics
Target acquisition
 slow down, 94
Tasco red-dot scope, 94
Teal Slam, 129
Telescopic sights. *See also* Optics
 advantage, 95-97
Television and video programs
 Peter Fiduccia, 6
Terrain
 vs. hunting strategies, 134
Three-or four-reed hand-stretched mouth call, 151
Thunderstorm. *See also* Poor weather conditions
 turkey hunting, 46
Tom Gaskins scratch box, 99–100
Topo map
 scouting, 18
  while hunting, 69
Tracking, 26
 electronic TrackMaster
  bowhunting, 80–81
 Game Tracker, 80–82
 ground scent, 168
 signs, 20
 track sign picture, 23
TrackMaster, 81
T.R.U. Ball Tornado release, 82–83
Turkey. *See also* Gobbling turkey; individual types

orient to water, 137
picture, 2, 3, 18, 53, 102, 112, 131, 143
recipes, 177–184
wounded
    dog assisted recovery, 169–170
Turkey and morels
    recipe, 180–181
Turkey calling. *See* Calling
Turkey camp stew
    recipe, 182–183
Turkey dogs, 163–176
    Appalachian Turkey, 165, 174
    assisting recovery
        wounded turkeys, 169–170
    barking, 175
    breeding dogs, 174
    Byrne, John, 174
    calling, 172
    Clare, Pete, 170–174
    English setter pointer, 174–175
    fall turkey hunting
        legal with dogs, 166
    Gerry Bethge, 168–169
    gundog men, 166
    mixture, 167
    Plott hound pointer, 174–175
    requirements, 167–168
    turkey hunting, 91
    woodsmanship, 172
Turkey hunters. *See* Hunters
Turkey Hunting Secrets, 13
Turkey pot pie
    recipe, 181–182
Turkey salad
    recipe, 183
Turkey target
    for patterning shotgun, 93
Turkey Trot Acres, 170

U
Unseasonable temperatures. *See also* Poor weather
        conditions
    gobbling periods, 52-54
    hunt effectively, 42
Uphill, 111–120

V
Video programs
    Peter Fiduccia, 6
Vision, 156
    human *vs.* turkey, 85–86
Voice and Vocabulary of the Wild Turkey, 108
Volume
    locator calls, 101

W
Wait 'em out
    later in season, 36

Wait 'em out (*continued*)
little gobbling activity, 36
nothing gobbling, 37
vs. run and gun, 31–40
Wait time, 34
Weather, 41–50. *See also* Poor weather conditions
gobbling periods, 52–54
hunting tactics, 36
Web site
TurkeyHuntingSecrets.com, 13
Whines
blinds, 70
Whitetail Strategies
Peter Fiduccia, 6
Wild hogs
hunt, 129
Tim Hooey, 7
Wildlife biologists
scouting, 19
Wild turkey recipes, 177–184
Wild turkey rice soup
recipe, 180
Williams, Lovett, 14–15
blinds, 67
calling, 108–109
henned-up gobblers, 57–58
last-ditch tactics, 158
picture, 15
scouting, 26–27
Williams's studies
carrying capacity, 171
Wind. *See also* Poor weather conditions
hunt effectively, 42
hunting tactics, 35–36
turkeys movements, 47
Wooden strikers, 107
Woodsmanship
turkey hunting dogs, 172
Woods N' Water
television series, 7
World Slam
defined, 130
Writers/authors
John McDaniel, 9
Lovett Williams, 14
Peter Fiduccia, 6
Roger Raisch, 13

Y
Yelps, 108
fall turkey hunting, 149
gobblers, 150
henned-up gobblers, 56
soft, 127
three times, 101
wait three hours, 32
Youngsters
blinds, 61–63